MW00875361

Advar

The Funny Thing About Forgiveness

"Andrea warmly and gently guides her readers through a method and mindset that will help create and deepen their connection with others. Her stories and examples reflect all facets of life and will inspire you to be the bravest and most generous version of yourself."

Chris Arnold, Chief Operating Officer, Fred Rogers Productions

"As a workplace inclusion scientist-practitioner, I'm always on the hunt for actionable tools my clients can use to foster more inclusive interactions and organizational cultures. This book equips inclusive leaders with strategies and examples about how to use improvisation to make others feel more valued, respected, seen, and heard—what inclusion is all about."

Dr. Victoria Mattingly, CEO Mattingly Solutions

Andrea's hilarious and inspiring take on workplace culture has the power to reshape our views on forgiveness and confrontation. A must-read for leaders who seek to connect more deeply with their team.

Luke Bennecker, Product Management Executive

This book is a breath of fresh air in what has been a very difficult two years. I have started reading it for the second time through so that this time I can stop and journal and do some of the heart and mindset work that Andrea leads us through in the book. The world needs more people with peace in their hearts; please read this book!

Pablo, USA Reader - Review taken from Amazon

"One of the teachings in *The Serving Leader* is that you get greatness out of people by expecting it. Andrea's book introduces mindful improv thinking as a means by which leaders can learn to genuinely expect greatness from themselves and others - especially after past failure. She shares a method for becoming authentic and consistent in your servant leadership by shifting how you forgive and confront yourself and those around you."

Kenneth R. Jennings, Internationally Bestselling Author of *The Serving Leader* and *The Greater Goal* & Co-Founder of Third River Partners

I was excited to read *The Funny Thing About Forgiveness* to learn how to apply principles of improv to leadership and building organizational culture. The book certainly delivered on that front with many valuable frameworks and examples that I plan to use in leading our organization and working with tech startup leaders. What I didn't expect was its personal impact - that it would help me gain clarity on current career challenges, increase my enjoyment of family vacations and provide the page-turning experience of a novel - feeling emotions of compassion, outrage, laughter and joy at Andrea's stories and optimistic view on people. There are so many reasons to recommend this book - perhaps the most important is the feelings of optimism and empathy that are at the core of its teachings - a powerful perspective that is so needed today in this increasingly polarized world.

Jim Jen, Chief Operating Officer, Innovation Works & Founding Managing Director, AlphaLab

"Irreverently funny and insightfully relevant, Andrea cuts to the heart of how readers contribute to the vicious cycle of dysfunctional communication. Her engaging, conversational style packs in punches of wisdom. By employing Andrea's methods in *The Funny Thing About Forgiveness*, readers can more fully embrace heart-centered leadership to their own benefit and the benefit of their colleagues."

Lauren Reed, Senior Director of Human Resources, Schell Games

"Leadership is about good listening. More importantly, it is about making sure the speaker knows they have truly been heard. Andrea's hilarious book overflows with practical guidance helping leaders use forgiveness and improv to make this happen in surprising and powerful ways."

Jim Kauffman, Ph.D., Leadership Development Consultant & Executive Coach

"This book is a must-read for the enlightened leader who is looking to inspire their team, lead by example and always put curiosity over judgement."

Priya Amin, Serial Entrepreneur & TEDx Speaker

"Being an effective leader requires overcoming obstacles, and we are often quick to call out the situations and people that we believe impede our progress. Andrea's hilarious and moving book teaches us that the F-word is not just some grand gesture we bestow on those who wronged us in profound ways, but a practice we can bring to our day-to-day interactions, confronting and overcoming the beliefs that are actually holding us back. *The Funny Thing About Forgiveness* has not only provided me with inspiration and techniques to get out of my own way, but also to be a better "scene partner" to the people in my life."

Mike Capsambelis, Founder & Trustee, Awesome Pittsburgh

"The word that resonates throughout this body of work is "Alignment". Alignment of self, of circumstance, of others, is a critical component in understanding the concept of forgiveness. Practicing the art of alignment is what Andrea's book so succinctly communicates."

Lisa Iadicicco, Executive Director, Women in Bio

"*The Funny Thing about Forgiveness* encourages all of us to be more present in our own story; to listen, be curious, and to forgive. Using illustrations from life and work, Andrea Flack-Wetherald brilliantly shows us in this book how Mindful Improv can create a more peaceful world. Highly recommend."

Chris Cooke, Consultant & Executive Coach

"You can't change the past, but you still have a say in what happens next" is perhaps one of the most poignant and memorable lines in a book filled with many poignant lines, and many memorable (and laughable) moments. Encouraging a deeper yes is the key takeaway that heart-centered leaders long to provide through reframing forgiveness in a moment, in a masterpiece, and in motion. Andrea offers clear processes, practical applications, and absolutely hysterical anecdotes! Pick this book up now--page through it, then dig in and get to work on the way that you approach the f-word in your own life.

Holly Joy McIlwain, Director of Human Resources, Robert Morris University; Founder, Brave Women Project & Author

This book provided me access to a secret formula used in improv. The best performance requires the team to enter the stage with no preconceived agenda, a trust of teammates, and through the power of "And Yes", build upon ideas as opposed to fault-finding. So read this book if you want to unlock the secrets of creating a sustainable synergistic culture.

James Jordan, CEO of StraTactic, Inc

"Reading *The Funny Thing About Forgiveness* gives me hope, but also courage. And courage, I am learning, is hope on-the-move. Andrea's words remind me to stay curious and that authentic "yes, and's" in both my personal and professional relationships, are the source of unmitigated possibility."

Liz Mims, Director of Client Services, Dress for Success Pittsburgh

Maybe it's because I started my career in the early 1990s, when women lacked representation in the C-suite and most board rooms in the booming tech industry. Or maybe it's those flashbacks from high school math and science class. You know the scene where the teacher ignores the female hands in the air to call on the chosen few brilliant young men who would go on to ivy league colleges and prestigious military academies. But my own personal improv stage was tainted from these early experiences, which created a sense of frustration and judgment as I worked hard to constantly prove myself throughout my career. Not until I spent some time with Andrea's book did I realize that it was these and other seemingly minor life experiences that shaped the way I navigate through my professional world. With this new lens, I am able to view every experience and interaction as a gift, as an opportunity for curious conversations that have the power to bring about true connection with my colleagues and help me lead with courage and love. Thank you, Andrea!

Jess Jordan-Pedersen, Chief Marketing Officer at RE2 Robotics

"Through my career as a woman in a male-dominated environment, I gained a Ph.D. shoving cutting words and toxic behaviors under the proverbial carpet. I only wish I had the insightful techniques presented in this book. Andrea's graceful way of navigating through challenges is not only shown in this book but presented as practical skills for us to follow.

In today's workplace environment where employees are more empowered than ever to choose the right culture, and EBRG's are not the one-stop solution, this book encourages us to take an honest look at ourselves and our inner wounds in order to become the best version of ourselves, and in that way, be the best leaders we can be.

This book is a must for any organizational leader looking to create an inclusive, collaborative, and thriving culture. I am for sure a new Yes, AND advocate!"

Dr. Neysha Arcelay, Bestselling Author & Founder, Precixa

THE FUNNY THING
ABOUT FORGIVENESS

THE FUNNY THING ABOUT FORGIVENESS

What every leader needs to know about improv, culture, and the world's least favorite F word

By Andrea Flack-Wetherald

Foreword by Colin Mochrie

www.andbeyondimprov.com/funnythingaboutforgiveness

Copyright © 2021 Andrea Flack-Wetherald

All rights reserved. This book may not be reproduced in whole or in part without written permission from the author, except by a reviewer who may quote brief passages in a review; nor may any part of this book be reproduced, stored in a retrieval system , or transmitted in any form or by any means, electronic, mechanical, photocopying, recording, or other without written permission from the author. Failure to comply with these terms may expose you to legal action and damages for copyright infringement.

ISBN: 9798759753681

Editor's note

The names and details have been changed in some stories to protect the privacy of those mentioned in this publication. This publication is not intended to be a substitute for seeking advice or evaluation from a health care professional.

Dedicated in gratitude and loving memory to Thelma & Lowell Nichols: my first examples of daily-life improvisers and two of my favorite human beings.

FOREWORD

By Colin Mochrie

When Andrea Wetherald asked me to write a foreword to her book, being the amazing improviser that I am, I said yes.

That was immediately followed by mild terror. I know nothing about writing a foreword. Who do I think I am, thinking I could preface this amazing book with my ramblings?

Then I realized I had to face the fear. I had to change my thinking. I had to consciously use a skill in life that I've been using unconsciously onstage. Follow me on my little ramble.

Improvisation has been very good to me. It gave me a career that didn't exist when I was growing up. Through improv I met my wife, many good friends, and got the chance to travel the world working with exceptional people. With all the positivity that it has brought to my life, it shocks me that it took so long for me to actually incorporate its tenets into my off-stage life. I wish Andrea's book had come out a few years earlier.

When I meet fans of Whose Line is it Anyway, I'm usually asked the same three questions. Is it really made up (YES), how do you remain so attractive (Hydration!) and isn't improv really hard to do? The difficult thing about the last question is that the answer is yes and no.

No, because we do it every day. Every conversation we have, every event through the days of our lives, is improvised. If everyone can do it, it must be easy, right? Not so fast. When it comes to improvising onstage, it becomes a little trickier.

The thing that people starting out in improv find difficult is that we have to use skills that we are not comfortable with in day-to-day life: listening, accepting ideas, building on them, and dispensing with your ego. An example:

Say I start a scene.

"It looks like these murders were committed by a homicidal chicken."

"Yes, initial tests show that it was probably a Rhode Island Red with anger issues."

The idea has been accepted and built upon. But if I come on stage ready to do my fantastic chicken idea and my partner starts the scene in a derelict space station, I have to drop my idea and accept and build on his. I have to drop my preconceived idea for the good of the scene.

Either one of those scenarios could soar or fail, but the point is that we are in the moment and working together to achieve our goal: to create a good scene.

My epiphany about using improv in my real life happened after teaching a corporate workshop. A team in this particular company was having difficulties working together. I came up with a two-hour format to teach "yes and," working together, etc. I spent the entire lesson just trying to get them to say yes.

In every scene, someone would propose something, and immediately it was shot down with a no, or a "I think we should…" or "I have a better idea." For two hours, the team refused to accept the simplest idea until someone said "yes" to an offer, and this lovely scene happened. It was right at the end of the class. The experience made me start to wonder if I actually *was* that negative in my own dealings with friends, family, and associates outside of being onstage. I was.

An example: my wife Deb is the love of my life. I cherish her and we have a happy and fun marriage. But I realized that I often went to the negative in some of our interactions. I would have a predetermined idea as to what she was about to say and how the situation would play out. And because of those limits that I gave myself, I did not give our relationship the respect it deserved.

With my newfound belief in using the power of improv in relationships, our union strengthened. When we would have a disagreement, I would enter the conversation with no expectations, I actually listened, and--this was the important one for me--I treated Deb in real life as I would treat her on stage: I trusted her.

This is a woman who has gone through the trenches with me, supported me unflaggingly, who fought to make our marriage the best one ever. So why would I head into a confrontation by making her the bad guy? Why would this partner all of a sudden try to derail our "scene"? Of course she wouldn't.

Suddenly the bumps in the road that all partnerships hit weren't as worrisome. I discovered that for many of our arguments, we were really on the same side: we just weren't listening properly. I then expanded this technique to family, friends and people I worked with and with great results.

Whether it was co-workers who I felt weren't listening to me, employers who intimidated me, or family members who would push my buttons, I started to mend, enrich and, in some cases, form a totally different and positive relationship than the one we had previously. Of course, being human, there are times where I fall back into my bad habits, but I do this less often than I did before.

Now we get to the point of this foreword: this book. Andrea's book deals with mindful improv, combining the joy of improv with exercises that will shift your behavior and bring peace, joy, and passion into all your endeavors both in and out of your workplace.

As someone who has worked as a behavior change coach for years, who better than Andrea to write this book, which will help us transform the way we interact with friends, co-workers, and loved ones. Her takes on how to deal with confrontation and manage conflict will help you understand forgiveness in a new way, and your relationships will benefit.

Imagine the world if people everywhere took these teachings to heart. Imagine a CNN panel actually communicating and listening to each other rather than shouting to get their preconceived ideas out. Imagine a G7 summit where countries worked together in a positive way to get to a positive conclusion. It seems too fantastical--but then again, so did a lot of things that we now take for granted.

Enjoy the book. Put all that you learn into practice, and I can guarantee that a whole new world will open to you. Hey, if I can change my behavior to do something as simple as writing a foreword, imagine the possibilities.

CONTENTS

GRATITUDE & ACKNOWLEDGEMENTS

This book would not have been possible without the incredible support and encouragement of my husband Kyle. Thank you for talking ideas out with me, for being so patient with this long and unpredictable process, and for graciously solo-parenting on the weekends I ventured away to write this manuscript. Thank you to my mom (Connie Flack) and my sisters Alyse Flack-Brown and Aimee Juarez for your relentless support, optimism, and belief in me and this work. Thank you to my dad, Ron Flack, for the example you've always set of intentional relationship building, freely asking sincere questions, and talking with all people like you believe they have something to teach you. I love you all so much.

Thank you to my agent, Angela Scheff, for your guidance, advice, thoughtful questions, and listening ear throughout this process. Thank you to Cathleen Falsani for your encouragement and honest feedback: your support means so much to me! Thank you to my dear friend and editor, Jennifer Locke, for encouraging me to be brave and for providing accountability at some critical moments in this journey. And for editing my book so it doesn't suck. That in particular is very helpful.

Thank you to Erin Kelly for sharing your insights as a trauma therapist and trusted friend through many conversations about forgiveness, resilience, release, and trauma recovery. This book wouldn't have been formed without our collaboration early on - the coffee is on me forever!

Thank you to my business coach, friend, and "big sister" Joy Bufalini for your encouragement, tactical advice and *example*. We get to build whatever we want to build in this life :)

Thank you to John and Milonica Stahl-Wert for your encouragement, advice, and cottage! Thank you to Aaron Tarnow for your assistance and pep talk when I was deciding whether or not I was brave. That phone call was a critical turning point for the existence of this book. Thank you to Colin for stepping out of your comfort zone and writing such a thoughtful foreword! I'm not sure I would have had the confidence to keep pushing forward with this project during a global pandemic without your early partnership. Thank you to Sean Mulvihill for reaching out to me two years ago and bringing so much applied improv goodness into my life. Thanks also for pushing me to just freaking self-publish already.

Thank you to the many wonderful improv teachers and coaches I've had over the years: Patricia, Greg, Ben K, Ben A, Jethro, Abby, Kasey, Justin, Karen, Chris, and many others. I'm so grateful for all of your feedback and notes that led to so much growth and self-discovery through improv. A special thank you to the folks at Arcade Comedy Theater who invited me to perform at their theater when I wasn't really sure what my next steps were as an improviser. Your universal timing was perfect, and there are so many pieces of my work and my story that wouldn't be possible without you. Thanks also to the many, many amazingly talented improvisers I've had the pleasure of learning from and performing alongside.

Thank you to Lynda, Jay, Lee Ann, Yvette, Carolina, Lisa and Bruce - your *frientorship* has been such a gift to me at various stages of my journey. I am so, so grateful for each of you. Thank you.

Thank you to incredible friends like Liz, Cornell, Casey, Salmon Alley (wink), Keri, Kristen, Candace and Nick for holding the light for me at challenging times in this process and in *life*. Thanks for the connections you've made for me, the questions you've asked at the perfect time, and the faith you've had when mine was dwindling.

Thank you to the leaders whose support has helped this book make a bigger impact than it could have ever made if it were just me working on this project.

When I think of you all, and the deep bench of amazing people I have in my life, my cup overflows.

INTRODUCTION

Forgiveness is the soft skill no one's talking about in corporate spaces. That's a real missed opportunity because forgiveness is what enables leaders to be who they mean to be consistently, and therefore create a culture that consistently matches their good intentions. It's what frees them from the distractions of shame, resentment and suspicion so they can build amazing things in this world and feel sincere *joy* while doing so!

As a society, and maybe even as a planet, we have a natural aversion to the word *forgiveness*. When we're angry, hurt, outraged or fearful, there's a different--less helpful–f word upon which we are inclined to lean. We have a complicated relationship to the word and idea of forgiveness because:

- We can think of times we felt pushed into it without choice
- We've been taught that "I forgive you" and "That's okay" are interchangeable
- We've experienced trauma and have valid justifications for the resentments we hold
- We've seen or experienced forgiveness as absolution without accountability
- It feels abstract, exhausting, and maybe even re-traumatizing
- It seems important but not urgent and certainly unrelated to our professional lives

But what if I told you forgiveness is NONE OF THOSE THINGS? What if I told you there's a whole new way to understand and engage with forgiveness, and that doing so is the most important leadership development work you could ever do?

5

More on that coming very soon, but first a story:

One time at Mennonite college, I ripped a hole in the seat of my jeans during chapel. I sat in one of the front rows and when I stood up, the whole auditorium could see my naked butt skin because I was wearing a black lacy thong…to Mennonite church. Something I now feel both fine and gross about. I mean, who cares what undies you're sporting to church? But also…why deal with a self-imposed wedgie anywhere, for any reason? Gross.

I tell this story so you know who you're dealing with: a thong-to-chapel-wearer who has shown her left butt cheek to at least 100 Mennonites.

I am other things too: a social worker turned improviser turned leadership and culture coach. I am a mom to two amazing kids. I am a lover of dogs, bonfires and pondering the universe with close friends and people I met like a second ago, but who are totally *there*. I am a woman of faith and a firm believer in the power of mindfulness practice and improvised comedy to change the world by changing the people who *lead*. I am all of those things… but the butt cheek exposure of 2007 somehow seems like a critical part of getting me.

It's also just an amuse bouche, because Butt Cheek Chapel Day is not the most cringe-worthy thing I did at Bluffton University.

In 2008 I was a sophomore (in years, and in the sense that means 'immature'), and Barack Obama was campaigning to become the first Black president of America. Even as someone surrounded mostly by Republicans, I could feel the excitement of this historic moment! His candidacy was creating a platform that lifted up so many underrepresented voices across America. For example, the people who believe an antichrist is coming, and have several blog posts and the book of

Revelation to back them up. Oh yes, these people exist! If you could time travel down Rt. 30 in eastern Ohio, you would see their spray painted particle board yard signs and you would know you're with my people.

On June 7th, 2008, Hillary Clinton dropped out of the race and Obama became the presumptive Democratic nominee. I was home from college at the time. When my mentor and church league volleyball coach reached out for an *immediate coffee meeting* in which he would share urgent information regarding one *Barack Hussein Obama*, I was available.

When I got to our local coffee shop, Dale (not his real name) greeted me with his trademark thousand-watt smile and a big hug. He bought me a latte and we sat for 30 minutes of laughter-filled, soul-affirming, catch-up-on-life conversation before we got down to business. Dale pulled out a folder containing timelines, Bible verses, news headlines and other damning evidence, categorically *proving* that Barack Obama was the Antichrist.

I don't know if it was the deliciousness of the lavender latte, or our shared years in the trenches of Nazarene volleyball … but rather than run for the hills as a sensible person would have done, I sat and asked follow-up questions. After all, I trusted Dale and God works in mysterious ways. Was I really going to *deny* a scriptural prophecy just because I didn't understand it completely? Was I really going to be rude to someone who had been a trusted friend of the family since I was a child?

So I stayed, and I listened. And after an hour, I believed him.

"Oh dag, Andrea. Don't beat yourself up about it. Lots of people get pulled into odd beliefs by people they trust! You were young and impressionable, and it's not like you EMAILED

THE STAFF OF YOUR COLLEGE INCLUDING THE PRESIDENT HIMSELF to further propagate this conspiracy theory."

…that's exactly what I did next. *The people need to know!* I thought heroically.

I sat down at my laptop, fueled by a sense of divine urgency and impending doom, and I typed the most *embarrassing email* of my life. "I better include links" I thought "After all, these are college professors who will want citations."

Because of mercy or technical malfunction (but probably mercy), nobody responded to this email.

I don't remember a specific moment of de-radicalization, but I do remember the look on my mother's face when I told her what I'd done, and the slow blanket of shame that enveloped me as I began to realize what a massive misstep that was.

That story was too shameful for me to admit to anyone for *years*: not even my closest friends. It felt so much bigger than an email. It cast a cloud of suspicion over the people in my home church: *they all know him. They all like him. They all buy insurance from him. Do they agree? Are they all pulled into this bizarre end times conspiracy obsession?* It cast a cloud of suspicion over my own judgement! *How could I have let that happen? How could I have gotten pulled into something so obviously untrue? How could I sacrifice common sense so easily?* I went on to build a career speaking in public… and I frequently imagined one of my professors showing up to an event with a print out of the email and telling everyone in the room *the truth* about who I really was.

That email positively haunted me.

Years later, while writing a sketch show called *Sacrelicious*, it occurred to me that I might find some peace by just airing my ugly secret publicly. *What if I just admit it out loud before anyone else can?* So I did. During the story telling portion of the show, I told a crowded comedy theater the thing I was most ashamed of… and I finally released my shame cloud.

…On that subject at least!

I've got an arsenal of ridiculous behavior to work through, but I now understand how to do it. I now understand how to be free from the shame storm and it's cousin: the self-righteous resentment storm. And in case you're worried, spilling your beans to a crowd of rambunctious comedy goers is *not* a requirement.

This is not a book about spilling your beans. It *is* a book about acknowledging your beans and coming to a new understanding of what to do with them. It's a book about forgiving yourself and the people around you. For big stuff and for little stuff. It's a book about reckoning with our stories and with the people around us through honorable, improv-inspired confrontation.

Most of us have very painful stories - maybe even deeply traumatic stories - and when we think about the need for forgiveness in our lives, it's natural to think about those most painful experiences first.

I was sexually assaulted in my church as a young child. The perpetrator went to jail, and so did I… in a sense. I was raised in that church, despite these events. For 15 years I sat through Sunday school lessons, memorized scripture and learned about *purity* (the most important thing a girl has in evangelical culture) in the same room where mine was stolen.

But what I've noticed in my life and in the lives of my clients is that the goldmine of opportunities for forgiveness to work it's freedom and focus creating magic are *not only housed in those most painful stories*. In fact, I have used the forgiveness techniques I teach in this book to work through small stuff that has unleashed very big freedom, joy, clarity and empowerment!

Once, I was teaching the Proactive Forgiveness Process – which you'll learn later in this book - to a coaching client who was in the process of starting a new company more than a decade after leaving her physically and emotionally abusive husband. Years had passed but feelings of shame and not-enoughness still lingered and prevented her from taking this next step in her career.

Between sessions, she decided go through the Proactive Forgiveness Process steps with her ex in mind, hoping that would relieve her of the self-doubt and insecurity slowing down her professional expansion. On our next call, she shared that *it didn't help at all*! She said that after years of therapy, she had already processed their relationship and had already forgiven him. "I'm not really sure if forgiveness work is what I need." She said.

Not so. Where there is doubt, shame, resentment, worry, indecision, wheel-spinning, stuckness or otherwise feelings of "ploppishness" as I sometimes call it – there is the need for forgiveness.

I realized we were starting from an incorrect baseline assumption: that her abusive spouse (AKA: her most painful and glaringly obvious forgiveness story) was the root of her wobbly confidence. Using a mindful improv curiosity exercise (also taught in this book), we uncovered that the true source of her self-doubt and insecurity was something small. So small it was hard for her to say it out loud to me. Some hot shot new guy in her department had made a short, dismissive comment during a staff meeting three years beforehand... and that short, dismissive comment cut deeply. It made her feel small. Inadequate. Obsolete.

For three years, a small thing had been the rock in her shoe - knocking at her confidence and validating her mental fear gremlins. For three years, a small thing caused her to nurse a grudge. A *small thing* caused her to feel lost in her career path: too young to retire, and too old to chase her dreams.

Being in that moment of discovery with her was such a delight and honor. We worked the proactive forgiveness steps with the correct situation in mind, and it was powerful.

In our culture, we have given each other permission to be hurt by traumatic events. We have evolved to understand trauma (more than before at least) and create space for the need for healing in those circumstances. ..but we cut each other at the knees when it comes to *daily forgiveness opportunities.*

We say "Don't sweat the small stuff." Or "That's not worth your time." Or "That person is beneath you."

And we don't realize the dreams or the impact we are sacrificing on the altar of the perceived emotional high road.

Your feelings aren't too small to matter. In fact, you are living with a cauldron of forgiveness opportunities that - when identified and processed- will yield joy, personal growth and leadership consistency that would never have otherwise been accessible.

Shame caused by unprocessed stories make us miss opportunities and cause unintentional harm--in life *and* in business.

I almost didn't write this book, because the first time I said the words "I want to be an author" out loud, the person I was on a date with said "Ha! *Everyone* has a book to write." I felt so small and so embarrassed: how foolish to think anyone would care what *I* have to say, and how embarrassing that I said it out loud with such naïve optimism. Even though that was our first and last date, his words are basically trapped in my dang amygdala forever.

Often when I sat down to write, I imagined him scoffing from the other side of my laptop. He was always staring at me over his thick-framed glasses with an unnecessary scarf wrapped around his perpetually cold neck, his coffee steaming in front of his tight lipped lizard mouth. (See? I'm a born writer).

It would have been SUCH a shame to miss out on the exciting, terrifying and wonderful experience of writing this book, because I took on someone else's fear and insecurity. (I mean, that dude for sure also wanted to be an author.) Had that unprocessed story rerouted me from writing this book, life would have gone on, but the point is that resentment, fear and shame are really horrible boat captains.

What does any of this have to do with leadership?

Ummm. Everything.

The most hurtful leadership behaviors are not necessarily committed by "bad leaders." They're committed by human beings whose unprocessed stories are driving the boat.

My goal as a heart-centered human is to allow purpose, wisdom, and love to drive the ship more often than fear, resentment, and shame. In this book, I share with you the practices I've put in place in my life to achieve that goal. I hope they are as meaningful for you as they have been for me!

This book invites purposeful Reflection and Reckoning. In this form of R&R, it's easy to get finger-pointy and name-call-y. When we recall our painful stories and how the shortcomings of ourselves and others contributed to those stories, we can be tempted to assign "shame labels" to everyone.

She is selfish. Or, *I am a bad leader.*

This is not helpful or necessary.

As the indelible Fred Rogers once sang "The very same people who are good sometimes are the very same people who are bad sometimes. It's funny but it's true. It's the same, isn't it, for me… Isn't it the same for you?"

Yes. Yes, it very much is.

I am a former peddler of conspiracy theories, present-day Mennonite improviser, and momtrepreneur who, in one moment, loses my shit over raw spaghetti noodles in the toilet; in the next, I equip heart-centered leaders to consistently be who they mean to be. I am good sometimes. I am bad sometimes.

WHAT YOU'RE ABOUT TO READ:

My goal in this book is to convince you of three things and empower you to implement them accordingly:

1. You are an amazing improviser, which is great news since all of life is improv. The answers for how to become a better leader, or how to course correct within your team or your organization's culture …or even the trajectory of your LIFE: you've got all of those answers. They'll become clear when you learn to embrace yourself as an improviser and tap into the critical improv skills that help improve your daily "scene work."

2. *Forgiveness is the path to effective leadership.* Proactive forgiveness is the most important leadership skill you can ever develop, because it's what enables you to trust yourself as an improviser, to trust the scene partners around you, and to build something with them that you're proud of--not just something you can tolerate.

3. Healthy culture is achieved *through* confrontation, not despite it. This kind of culture which embraces relationship-building confrontation is only possible when we approach conflict with a forgiveness-first mindset.

My hope is that the ideas and practices in this book will bring you peace, and that they'll help you align with your truest, most loving self. That is the formula for strong leadership. I'm more convinced of the power of aligned leaders than I am of anything else in the world, including my conviction that Amy Grant is the greatest living musician of all time. And I'm VERY convinced about that.

Without further ado: here we go. Commence book.

CHAPTER 1: THE CORE FIVE

*"Life is improvisation. All of those [improv] classes
were like church to me. The training had seeped
into me and changed who I am."*

~ Tina Fey

*"We created 'theater of the heart' - a theater where people cherish each other
to succeed on-stage. Tell the students -
'theater of the heart.'"*

~ Del Close

When I have the privilege of introducing groups to improv for the first time as an event speaker or as a leadership coach, there are a few key bases to cover every time.

Base 1: Improv is different than stand up or sketch. Sketch and stand up often draw from improv for script writing, or as a means of ensuring the content stays fresh, but improv is completely made up *in its entirety.* From the moment an improv team is introduced on stage to the moment they leave, everything that happens is unscripted and completely inspired in the current moment.

Base 2: Why does this matter for your purposes? Because the same exact skills that make improv successful on stage make people successful off stage, too. When we cannot rely on scripts or carefully rehearsed delivery to make the audience laugh, the only way to achieve something of comedic value is to *rely on each other.*

Base 3: The anchoring philosophy of improv. When you first learn about improv, the words "Yes, and" will come up almost immediately. *Yes, and* is the basis of improv--it's the concept that helps us build improv scenes in the most foundational sense. "Yes, and" means: say "yes" to the information your scene partner has just contributed AND add your own piece.

In the years I've been bringing improv to corporate settings, I've felt a palpable tension when I get to this "third base" (You pervert! Get your mind out of the gutter!). The words "yes and" can sound trite or idealistic. After all: "In the *real* world, we can't say yes all the time."

I hear that objection often, and there is so much more to this concept than initially meets the ear. For this reason, I've started teaching *Yes, And* a little differently. More on that in the next chapter.

There are bounteous examples of improv skills that help us perform better at work and in life. These are the Core Five I point to most often, and the five I believe have the most dramatic impact on shifting the way we engage forgiveness, and therefore everything else that matters in leadership and life:

1. Choose Curiosity Instead of Judgement

2. Honor Your Scene Partner

3. Stay in this Present Moment

4. Listen Beyond Your Comfort Zone

5. Receive Everything as A Gift

Mindfulness practice is just being present in the current moment and exploring whatever is happening in your heart, mind, or surroundings with curiosity instead of judgement. Do you see some overlap with the list above? Improvisers are practicing the heart of mindfulness without even realizing it! Improv teachers are keen on saying things like "Don't think!" "What does your scene partner see here?" or "Don't try to save it!" These could also be heard as "Clear your mind. Stay curious. Don't judge what is happening. It's safe to accept things as they are."

Improv is a delightfully fun way to practice mindfulness! Let's take a deeper dive into the Core Five Skills and see how they set the foundation for embracing forgiveness, confrontation, and leadership differently.

Choose Curiosity Over Judgement

I love this one. We don't always understand *why* our scene partner is doing what they're doing, but our brains are pretty quick to start writing a narrative, aren't they?

Someone interrupted you? *It's because I'm a woman. Sexist!*

One sentence email reply? *Rude and uncaring.*

Left his dishes in the office sink? *Typical! Probably grew up with a silver spoon in his little one-percenter baby mouth!*

Once when I lived in Pittsburgh, I was driving up a steep, narrow road in the East End when a small herd of turkeys ran out in front of my car. I swerved and slammed the brakes to avoid hitting them. I was driving a stick shift on this steep, narrow hill, and of course I stalled out whilst sitting whompy-jawed in the middle of the road.

Just then a truck came around the corner, and the look on the driver's face was one of utter disgust. He blasted his horn and threw up his hands as I gestured wildly at the turkeys (which had all run into the bushes and were no longer visible) and tried to start the car. When I got the car going and finally got out of his way, I started cracking up.

HE DIDN'T SEE THE TURKEYS! And of course, the man didn't assume there was a turkey issue, because we were in the middle of a city.

Moral of the story: sometimes people do things we don't understand, because they've just had a turkey encounter. And other times it's because of their own unprocessed stories. Sometimes we really *are* seeing evidence of our scene partner's need for growth in some area... but mindful improv encourages us to ask: how can I build here? What might be going on? What turkeys might be hiding in the bushes?

This is where grace and brave questions work wonders!

On stage, the *choose curiosity over judgment* skill is required frequently. (At least for me. I'm kind of a judgy-pants. My Myers-Briggs is ENFJ with an emphasis on J FOR JUDGING.) Since improv is all made up, it's easy for the performers not to be on the same page. If I don't understand what's happening on stage, I've learned how to notice and shift away from my judging thought-traps: "Why is this person even on the team?" or "This idea is dumb - I can't wait for this scene to be over."

Those are counterproductive, joy-stealing, inner-peace-destroying thoughts.

Perhaps my scene partner was inspired differently by the audience suggestion; perhaps they simply misheard the suggestion (or perhaps *I* misheard!); perhaps their mom is in the audience and they're feeling a deep sense of urgency to prove themselves and this hobby worthy of respect and appreciation; perhaps this "proving energy" has caused them to make ill-advised scene-building choices (as proving energy *always does*).

What will help you build something you're proud of in the moments when you do not understand your scene partner's choices or behavior is to *proactively choose* curiosity instead of judgement. It gets you nowhere to stand on the sidelines judging their decisions, or second guessing the basis of your relationship. **Every moment you spend judging instead of deciding to get curious is a moment you've invested in the divide instead of in the relationship.**

Can you see how this improv tenet applies to real life? When you're faced with a perspective that you find shocking, or even appalling, it's decision time: do you choose the comfort of self-righteousness, where you can easily come to all kinds of conclusions about this person's integrity or value? Or do you choose curiosity?

What does my scene partner see that I don't? What must they believe or perceive about the situation to have drawn these conclusions?

Getting sincerely curious will help you start asking the questions that fuel productive conversations. The next time you're in this situation, try this question: "Can you help me see your point of view here?"

As we'll explore thoroughly in the Forgiveness chapters, the *curiosity over judgement* skill is also critical for turning inward and reflecting on our own behaviors with gentleness and self-compassion. This skill is imperative for engaging the proactive forgiveness process in a healthy and productive manner.

Maintain Faith in Your Scene Partner

This is a toughy. When you have a professional or personal relationship with someone, history has likely provided you opportunities to see that person "get it wrong" (whatever "it" is)…and vice versa. You've seen each other make mistakes, say hurtful things, and behave in ways that didn't capture the fullest picture of who either of you intended to be.

Del Close, often thought of as the father of improv as we know it, is quoted as saying "If we treat each other as geniuses, poets, and artists, we have a better chance of becoming that on stage." I've heard several variations of this quote (because I'm sure he said it different ways a lot of times!)—one iteration, which I haven't been able to verify on the internet, goes like this: "Your scene partner is a creative genius, but it's up to you to see them that way."

I love this. I love it so much. The deep truth about who your scene partner really is doesn't change, whether or not you go to the effort of seeing them that way.

The truth is, *we miss so many opportunities* to connect authentically with the people around us if we cannot give them the grace to believe they are more than the worst things about them. We are all more than the worst things about us.

Treat your scene partner like a creative genius, and you'll give them space to show you that they are. Treat your scene partner like a backwards, ignorant, asshole and you'll give them space to show you that they are.

People can feel whether or not you have faith in them. In more ways than we realize, we give people permission to manifest different parts of who they are in front of us.

Our expectations draw out our experiences. If we choose to see the positive, surprising, lovely, delightful aspects of our scene partner, we give them space to courageously show us the best versions of themselves.

Who people really are is *beautiful*. If you're not seeing beauty, you're seeing the crusty outer shell they've developed to protect themselves. Give them some grace; give them some faith... and you just may find that your scene partner was more than you realized all along.

Stay Focused in the Present Moment

The present moment is where magic and the possibility exist. What happened before is dead weight, and what could happen in the future is being determined *right now*. So pay attention!

When we feel resentment, that's an indication that we're stuck in the past. When we feel anxiety, that's an indication that we're stuck in the future. But when we feel *curiosity*, we're motivated to explore this current moment. The skills of choosing curiosity over judgment, maintaining faith in our scene partners, and staying present are all deeply intertwined. The "stay present" skill is especially critical when we're engaging vulnerable moments of conflict.

Firstly, the ability to participate in the Yes, And process depends on your ability to hear what's happening *right now*. You cannot add something meaningful and helpful if you haven't been listening to what's currently happening.

Secondly, present-moment focus helps us find creative endurance.

It's not uncommon for me to work with teams who are quite convinced that one or several teammates need to be fired. The advice I give my clients is this: Even if you're right that this person shouldn't work here in the long run, *right now they do.* Right now, this is your scene partner, and the onus is on both of you <u>equally</u> to do good work.

If doing good work with a "problem" colleague feels impossible, it's because you're not committed to the present moment--you're too caught up in the past or the future. You're either tangled up in memories of their past failures, or tangled up in hypothetical concerns about the future.

The truth is that *we find what we're looking for* in a given moment. Ain't that just the darnedest, most frustrating reality of life?

We think what we see around us is objective fact, but it's really a reflection of the story we tell ourselves, which determines what we're looking for. Each of us creates a narrative about our lives and the people surrounding us, and *if we're not careful, we can get more committed to that story than to the process of building what we actually want.* When we're committed to our stories, we create more and more of the *past* instead of creating the future we envision.

This is true in every circumstance: in our families, offices, communities, and intimate relationships. If you feel overwhelmed with negativity, it's because you keep looking for negative things to validate your negative perspective.

A simple shift in desire, from *validate my perspective* to *participate in what is good and helpful*, will help you break this cycle. Getting rooted to the present moment is one of the best ways to make that shift.

Listen Beyond Your Comfort Zone

There's not a ton of obvious overlap between my life as a Mennonite and my life as a comedian and improviser.

Perhaps this isn't shocking information. I bring it up because "listening beyond my comfort zone" is the only reason you're reading this book, instead of one called *For Three Days I Tried Improv, and It Was Terrible*.

As an improviser, an early lesson I needed to learn was that stepping out of a scene because something made me uncomfortable was a total cop out. And believe me, there were *plenty* of opportunities for me to learn this lesson.

Entering the world of comedy felt like earning a second college degree, only this time I wasn't learning about Human Behavior in the Social Environment; I was learning how the cool kids debaucher-ize on the weekends, and all the codewords for sex and drug-related activities. It turns out, there are *many* types of adult sexual relationships one can enter into of their own free will (who knew?). Two critical lessons I feel obligated to pass along, one I learned offstage and the other learned on:

When you learn a new thing from a comedian, it's best to ask a trusted friend *before* you Google it. Seriously. Ask first. There are things you cannot unsee.

Leaving or not listening in a scene because you are uncomfortable is really about your own fear, and it's tied to an underlying belief that *other people* are controlling the direction of the scene. The truth is, every improviser is equally responsible for the direction of the show through their creative contributions. You can't change the past, but you still have a say in what happens next.

This revelation was deeply impactful to me. First of all, I reflected on the number of off-stage scenes (in college especially) I exited rather than engaged. (I exited because I was uncomfortable, or perhaps I was feeling a bit self-righteous.) Secondly, I realized that every utterance from your scene partner's mouth is not necessarily thought-through, purposeful, or intended to direct the rest of the scene. It's not always pointing at some deeply-rooted desire or resentment.

Sometimes people say things that just come out wrong. We need grace for that! *We all need grace for the journey.* Sometimes we need a healthy confrontation with our scene partner; other times, ignoring and moving on is the best "yes, and."

LISTENING HYGIENE

Yeah, that's right. Listening is so important that this skill gets its own subchapter title.

When I teach my clients about listening, I never talk about "listening skills." I teach them about *listening hygiene*.

A "skill" is something that can be learned and internalized so well that eventually it becomes second nature. Playing an instrument is a skill; riding a bike or driving a stick shift are also skills. When we perform a skill, our brains can check out and muscle memory can take over.

Not so with listening. Listening is more like *bodily hygiene*. I vaguely recall learning about *hygiene* in my sixth grade health class. We talked about the difference between deodorant and antiperspirant, and that's all I remember, because I knew we were about to talk about sex, and let's be serious: that was the only thing I wanted to hear about[1].

Perhaps you paid more attention than I did, but regardless: you don't learn about the importance of hygiene in sixth grade health class and get to be instantly clean forever! If we've learned nothing else from Jonathan Van Ness (and we've learned plenty else from you, baeee!! Love you!!), we've learned that grooming and hygiene require proactive effort.

If we get lazy about our hygiene, the natural way of things is that our bodies will look unkempt and start to develop unpleasant odors. It does not mean something is wrong with us. In fact, it means our bodies are functioning as designed!

I remember what it was like when kids came into our family. We are a foster-adoptive family, and our kids came when they were 18 months and three and a half. Going from no kids to two toddlers, each with some extra needs, after a phone call from a case worker and only 45 minutes to prepare was *difficult*.

At one point, I was *four days* sans shower. Shaving? HA. Deodorant? HA.

One day, I stopped myself mid-rummage as I searched our dirty laundry hamper for my least dirty undies. When I realized the horror of what I was doing, I cried; then I called a friend to watch the kids so I could shower and do some damn laundry.

---

[1] Just for fun, you should know that the Christian school where I learned about sex in the sixth grade was *so* vague on the details that I didn't actually understand the mechanics of what sex was until I was 18 years old. How did I learn? *Not the fun way*. My boss at Chick-Fil-A drew a diagram on a napkin for me, because she felt ethically obligated to keep me from going to college without a clear understanding of how it works. Thanks, Chick-Fil-A! ... and all the people said: *my pleasure*.

Here's the take-home point--chaos (of the internal or external varieties) opens the door for a decline in hygiene. It's this way for our physical hygiene *and* our listening hygiene. So often when I enter into the workplace chaos alongside my clients, they spend a lot of time defending themselves for the inconsistencies between "how it is" and how they mean for it to be.

There is no judgement or shade from this hamper-rummager!

The point is NOT that you're doing something wrong. The point is that you'll feel better, connect better, and have better results that matter to *you* when you have some infrastructure in place to get your hygiene back on track.

Why is listening so hard when our bodies are designed to do it?

Part of the problem is that there's *so much noise* in the world today; at any given moment, there are six or 10 or 14 ever-present mobile apps vying for your attention. But I wonder if another problem is that we take listening for granted.

I've heard it said that there are four primary types of communication: reading, writing, speaking, and listening. Of those, *listening* is the only one that is not taught proactively in school.

We assume *listening* is a given, because *hearing* is one of our five natural senses, so we don't really build that skill. But for some people, it's not! Have you ever had the opportunity to learn about listening from the Deaf Community?

In high school, I took an American Sign Language (ASL) class which afforded me the privilege of learning a bit more about Deaf culture and communication. I really enjoyed it, and joined the ASL club, too! More recently, I've been inspired by the proactive and intentional nature of American Sign Language all over again through a family at our church whose young son is deaf[2].

Let me tell you: people who rely on sign language have *exceptional* listening hygiene. Here are some of my observations:

In sign language (at least in ASL), facial expression and eye contact are just as important as the signs themselves. Deaf people are masters of what makes up the *majority* of human communication: nonverbal cues.

The value of candor: when you put more effort into the words you pass along from your brain to another's, there's less filler content. You say what you mean, and do so directly.

Attention Captivation: guess how many Deaf couples communicate about something that matters to them while their scene partner is texting, watching something get unboxed on YouTube, or scrolling through pictures of baby otters on their phone? Zero. The obvious understanding is: if you're not looking at me, you're not *hearing* anything I'm saying at all.

When you sign, you *pay attention*.
Most people have taken enough classes, or watched enough TED talks, to know what active listening is. Active listeners pay attention to their body language, ask engaging questions, and

---

[2] Did you know that capitalization matters a lot when it comes to deafness? Capital "D" denotes Deaf culture and people who are a part of Deaf culture. Lowercase "d" denotes the adjective or noun of deafness itself, or deaf people who are not a part of the Deaf community (for example, this could be the case when deafness happens in adulthood as the result of an injury or illness, or when a child of hearing parents is born or becomes deaf).

are purposeful in how they schedule their time and where they have important conversations.

I often remind my clients that your knowledge on a subject is never a substitute for folks' lived experience of what it's like to communicate with you day in and day out. If there's extra chaos in your life, go to the extra effort of cultivating good listening hygiene. If you haven't been proactive about that, chances are you're not listening at the caliber of your intention.

Receive Everything as A Gift

In improv there are no mistakes. Well, perhaps more accurately, there are plenty of *mistakes*, but there are no *deal breakers*. There's nothing that could happen that would make a way forward impossible. We treat every single thing that happens as a *gift*.

As a Mennonite, this improv skill has a special place in my heart. It reminds me of an old hymn that says "Nothing is lost in the eyes of God; nothing is lost forever. God sees with love and that Love will remain holding the world forever.[3]"

I interpret this, with full sincerity, as a direct call to action as an improviser--on stage and in life. If I see with love (instead of self-righteousness, judgement and proving-energy), that love will hold the scene together.

A lot can happen when you enter into a live performance experience, especially one with no script or plan! Bottles break, audiences heckle or give purposefully uncomfortable

---

[3] *Nothing is Lost on the Breath of God* by Colin Gibson. Published in the Mennonite songbook *Sing the Story*; #121

suggestions[4], smoke detectors go off...I've even been kicked in the face!

More to the point, misunderstandings happen between players as we maneuver through improvised scenes without cues for entrances, exits, blocking, or space work. It's easy to misunderstand when someone is trying to end one scene to move into another. Sometimes we jump backwards and forwards in time on stage, and not all players make the leap! Awkward things are said. Heavy, hard-to-watch scenes get initiated – scenes the audience doesn't want to see and the improvisers don't want to be in.

Basically, shit can happen... and then the improvisers get to decide if it's shit, or if it's the perfect thing pointing them in the direction of what can happen next.

The invitation of improv is to decide that *nothing is a deal breaker;* that our creativity doesn't stop in the same place as our comfort zone.

THE CRITICAL REFRAME

Combining these tenants of improv was the impetus for the way I forever teach confrontation, both internal and external. Internal confrontation is a key part of the forgiveness process I teach later in this book, and external confrontation is an important part of how we allow the work we're doing *inside* to manifest in our families, work places, and social circles.

---

[4] If you go to an improv show, don't heckle. Save that noise for the stand-ups :)

But confrontation has such a bad rap! Therefore, I've used the mindful improv skills just described as the basis for this reframing exercise.

When I work with clients, I ask them to shout out examples of the words they use to describe confrontation. Usually the subsequent list includes:

- Eruption
- Explosion
- Getting shot down
- The shit hitting the fan

Before I started being more thoughtful on this subject, I used to describe heated or confrontational meetings at work as a "crap circus."

Our phrases describing external confrontation evoke images ranging from the violent to the apocalyptic to the disgusting. We don't have as many descriptors for internal confrontation-- probably because we avoid it so much!--but I have heard people talk about "shame spirals" or "re-traumatizing experiences" or "beating a dead horse." (All of the practices I share in this book are intentionally designed for your internal confrontation experiences NOT to be like that.)

None of those adages are helpful, especially if we hold true the understandings of *attention mechanics*, or the idea that our focus determines our experience. So if we're focusing on the negative, detrimental aspects of something, that will be our experience.

Instead, I encourage my clients to start thinking of confrontation like a piñata:

Something that has been hanging over our heads has received some focused, forceful momentum. It burst open and then *gifts fell from the sky.*

That is also what happens in confrontation! *Gifts are falling every which way.* Confrontation means it is literally raining opportunities to build on something that matters, to notice someone else's perspective, to connect on a deeper level, to improve a process that has been needing our attention... but it's the job of a good improviser (and you, my friend, are a very good improviser) not to miss those gifts because of the presentation or the wrapping paper.

Let's make our piñata analogy work a little harder. Imagine for a moment that you're a kid experiencing a piñata for the first time at a birthday party. It's a beautiful summer day, and you're running around a grassy backyard with fifteen other kids. You're enjoying the party with thoughts of cake and ice cream dancing through your head, when you notice an adorable paper mâché creature sitting near a tree.

"What an adorable little donkey," you think to yourself. *"I never would have thought to use all those beautiful colors to make a donkey! This is clearly the work of a creative and whimsical person."*

No sooner do you have this thought than a party guest begins tying a rope around the little guy and hoisting him onto a tree limb.

"Hmm...This family expresses appreciation for art differently than my family," you may think.

And then you see the family gathering around a blindfolded child with a baseball bat. They begin rooting and chanting for the child, and it becomes clear that nothing good is in store for that piñata.

Your hesitance has likely turned into panic by now.

"That child is going to destroy this work of art! I can't watch!" And you turn away to avoid witnessing the barbaric behavior unfolding before you.

If that's where you check out, what are you missing?! You don't see the gifts falling all around. You don't see the children preparing to find treasures and store them in their gift bags.

Now imagine an hour passes and you continue to run around this backyard party in your bare feet. Imagine running over to "the scene of the crime" out of sheer curiosity, and stepping on a piece of unclaimed piñata debris; perhaps a kazoo, or broken jolly rancher, or a toy soldier with a parachute.

Does that feel like a treasure, or a booby trap?

If this happens, you will leave that party thinking piñatas are the dumbest, most traumatizing and unnecessary birthday experience ever.

But that's not the experience the other children had! The difference is in your *expectation* and your *attention*. What could otherwise be received as a gift feels like a painful booby trap-- if you didn't know to look for the gift.

It's the same in confrontation; if you expect it to be helpful, it will be. If you expect to find valuable information you can use for continuing to build with your scene partner, you will. But if you disengage because it's uncomfortable, you'll miss the gift. The debris will still be there, however, and what could otherwise have been a powerful opportunity for connection can become a sharp point of contention.

Let's change the way we think about confrontation! Expect it to be the birthplace of authentic, meaningful relationships. Expect confrontation to be the perfect opportunity to build your vulnerability and empathy muscles. Expect it to point you to where growth and innovation can happen.

Confrontation will be what you let it be, so let it be helpful. You will find what you're looking for, so look for hope. You'll get what you expect, so expect a piñata instead of a crap circus.

When you see an opportunity for internal or external confrontation arising, it is my hope that you'll never again use the old fear-based adages to describe what's coming. Instead, I hope you'll dig into your mindful improv skills, put on a party hat, and break out a gift bag. *It's party time!*

MY FAVORITE PIÑATA STORY

There are relationships that only exist in my life because of this reframe.

About five years ago, I left an improv rehearsal in tears because a teammate lashed out at me unexpectedly. I'm a sensitive person, and as a new part of the improv community, this surprising, hurtful, and embarrassing situation had me telling a story that I should just quit.

"I don't really fit in with anyone," I told my husband.

As a former Evangelical and present-day Mennonite, I felt entirely out of place anyway. I was in my early twenties and married already. I had an extremely low alcohol tolerance and understood exactly zero of the jokes about bizarre sex stuff. Also, I spent all of the nineties at Jesus camp, and couldn't keep up with any of the pop culture references.

When my teammate lashed out at me, I immediately interpreted this as a sign that I simply didn't belong. *Why are you even here?* was my imagined subtext.

My husband encouraged me not to quit, so I went to rehearsal again the following week. Our team went out for drinks afterwards--a situation that always left me feeling insecure and out of place. (I had only recently learned that all alcohol was not called beer... so you know, I had very little in common with my urbane, cocktail-savvy counterparts.)

As we talked, the subject shifted to one of my favorite coaches, Chris. He was *everyone's* favorite coach because of his constant encouragement and inclusion of new improvisers. As improvisers often do in social situations, we started playing an absurd conversational game that had us laughing louder than may have been ideal for the restaurant staff at Fuel and Fodder. This time we were one upping each other on outlandish compliments for Chris.

Yay! I thought. *I have things to add to this conversation! I love Chris. Chris is the best!*

After several rounds of my teammates' compliments, it was my turn. "Chris is only barely *not* Jesus," I said emphatically.

Poking fun at my religious roots had become a safety net for me: it was an unavoidable difference, so why not embrace it?

We laughed… and then things took an unexpected turn.

Time has erased my exact memory of how the conversation devolved so quickly, but I remember winding up in the surprising and precarious position of defending my understanding of how the Bible was canonized.

I remember thinking "Why is this happening? I don't actually care *at all* what anyone believes about the Bible. I don't even know what *I* believe about the Bible! I didn't mean to make this a thing!"

But it was too late. The same teammate who had lashed out at me before was armed with facts and statistics and was happily putting me in my place.

Another improviser maneuvered the conversation to safer ground, and I sat there silently, biting back tears, until the group decided to disband for the evening. To be clear, part of the reason I was so hurt is that this teammate was one of my first improv friends. She was definitely *more* than how she was acting in that moment, but somehow her kindness in other situations sharpened the knife for this one.

I'm definitely quitting, I thought on the way home. *Why did I say that? I'm so embarrassed. I don't know how to relate with anyone at this theater. Everyone probably agrees with her; they'll probably be relieved if I just quit.*

I went home and talked it over with Kyle. Instead of jumping on the "How dare she?!" bandwagon, or agreeing that it was best to just walk away, Kyle reminded me of *the third way*.

See, Mennonites are *pacifists*, which actually means a lot more than our ability to be conscientious objectors during war time. Pacifism means that we don't participate in violence, but we also don't hide from conflict. We look for *the third way*. Not fight, not flight; something in the middle.

"I think you should talk to her," he said.

So for several days, I worked up the confidence to reach out. Then, on May 3, 2015 at 11:58 am (the joy of email communique), I sent the following email:

Hi <friend>,

Would you be willing to get coffee or drinks with me sometime in the next couple of weeks? I know we're both super busy, but there's something that's been bothering me since the last time we hung out and I just wanted to come to you directly and talk to you about it. I like you so much and absolutely love improvising with you! I don't want to feel weird the next time we're together so I just wanted to tell you that my feelings were hurt and I would love to talk with you about it if that's okay.

What happened next remains one of my most favorite examples of love in the world. I was immediately met with an understanding, receptive, kind-hearted person who sincerely wanted to build a relationship with me, too. Our email exchanges and follow-up face-to-face conversation were transformational for both of us.

When we talked, my teammate opened up about what was happening in her world. She was so brave, vulnerable, and sincere. She shared her story with me, and explained how stuck and lost and overwhelmed she was feeling.

I referred her to my therapist, who had been helping me through some of the challenges I was facing, and my own feelings of being stuck, lost, and overwhelmed. My friend was able to get the support she needed to consistently be her beautiful self. A couple of years later she shared a bit about this on social media, and said that this exchange "Literally changed/saved my life."

And lest you think the growth was one directional; I left the conversation that day with a worldview that had been completely blown open. I also left with the very first building blocks of what would eventually become *The Yes And Confrontation Flow*--a flow chart for effective confrontation, which I use with clients who are working to bring their culture into consistent alignment with their values.

The fact that I went from having an acquaintance to having a soul-level friend started me thinking...how often in the past have I reduced someone to a snippet of their behavior? How readily have I assumed my resentments were justified without giving someone the same grace that others have given to me when I needed it?

How many of these powerful, connective moments have I missed out on because I avoided the conversations that could have brought about this level of authentic, human connection... because I avoided saying the vulnerable words "my feelings were hurt?"

Those are such difficult words for grown adults to say. Yet so often, the vulnerability of being honest about hurt feelings will open a door you may not have even realized was shut.

To this day, my friendship with this person is one of my most treasured relationships. She is my kids' favorite babysitter, and both of my children want to marry her. Understandably so; she's pretty great.

I'm not saying that this magical degree of connection is the guaranteed outcome *every time*, but I am saying that *our scene partners cannot surprise us if we don't give them the opportunity.*

CHAPTER SUMMARY

The same anchoring truths of improvised comedy are true in life, because *we're all improvising all the time.* Every single person who reads this book is an improviser, regardless of how much stage experience you have. You've been improvising since your very first, infantile impulse to connect with the people around you, and every moment since.

Mindful improv lays the ground work for everything I teach about forgiveness. Mindful improv completely changes our experience of forgiveness and confrontation, both internally and externally.

We can stop using catastrophic analogies for confrontation. Think of confrontation as a piñata; when you see confrontation brewing, *get ready for gifts.*

You find what you're looking for, so look for what you need to make a situation better!

The Core Five improv skills for building more authentic relationships and facilitating more effective dialogue amidst disagreement are:

- Choose Curiosity Over Judgement
- Maintain Faith in Your Scene Partner (*your scene partner is a creative genius*)
- Focus on the Present Moment (*your invitation to join the magic is being offered right now*)

- Listen Beyond Your Comfort Zone (*listening hygiene*)
- View Everything as a Gift (*anything and everything can be used as a building block for connection*

CHAPTER 2: A NEW UNDERSTANDING OF YES, AND

"Everything handed to you is a gift. Saying no to this gift is denying the possibility of something magical happening. Still, no matter what character is handed to you, you can make strong choices on how you wish to play that character. You are in control. Keep your integrity high. Don't allow yourself to feel like a victim on-stage."

~ Charna Halpern in *Art by Committee*

I've heard some surprisingly intense philosophical debates on exactly what "Yes, And" means. A baseline understanding is: agree with what your scene partner offered, and add something of your own. But especially around the time when the #MeToo movement was on the rise, lots of female improvisers were re-evaluating what *yes and* means to us: on stage and off stage.

I was lucky enough to work at a theater where my (white male) improv coach--who was also one of the theater owners-- created space for my team to talk about this openly. The female members of the team were given a safe place to share our experiences and express our needs and concerns, so we could be our most creative and vulnerable selves *safely*.

We arrived at a collective understanding that *we do not have to say yes to everything* in order to "yes, and" effectively. "Yes, And" does NOT equal a sense of obligation to allow more of what you *don't* want to overtake a scene, or to *actively* build more of it for the sake of "being a team player." *In improv, saying "yes" does not equal being a doormat.*

Charna Halpern[5] shares a fantastic example of this in her book *Art by Committee*. She writes "I recall a performance when a woman was on stage. Two men entered, and the first man said 'Honey, I brought a friend home for dinner.' The woman's reply was, 'That's fine dear, but I asked you to call me Madam President when we are not alone.' There is always a way to control your own fate in your scene."

I love it! Yes, I am your wife and you've surprised me with another mouth to feed at dinner time. AND I am the President of these United States, and you'll address me as such while we ask the staff to make another plate.

You see, an improv "yes, and" is more than *agreeing* with whatever has just been said. In our world, "agree" means "acknowledge and accept" what your scene partner just contributed. Even if it's awkward, dark, a non sequitur, or otherwise not what you want.

To *yes, and* in those moments is to acknowledge what has happened rather than to avoid or ignore. To *yes, and* in those moments is to accept that what has happened created an impact--it exists now, and there are implications because of this.

"Yes, and-ing" is imperative for heart-centered leaders ALWAYS, but especially at this moment in history, when

---

[5] Charna Halpern is a formidable figure in the world of improv training. She taught many of the most recognizable names in comedy: Tina Fey, Amy Poehler, Bill Murray, John Belushi, Cecily Strong, Chris Farley, Gilda Radner, Mike Myers and the list goes on. In her impressive tenure as an improv teacher, she heard the frustrations of many female improvisers who felt type-cast and limited by the character initiations bestowed upon them by their male counterparts. The advice she offers for both coping and moving the art forward in *Art by Committee* has both challenged and encouraged me as performer on and off stage.

employees are begging to be heard. They are begging for leaders to acknowledge and accept--to *yes, and*-- the reality of current and historical events and the implications they have in the here and now.

To truly *yes, and* requires more than diversifying the leadership team and requiring DE&I training (although those are great things to do). A surface-level response leads to unintentional-- but still hurtful-- tokenization and performative action. To truly *yes, and* requires a commitment to stay in the scene even when it's uncomfortable; supporting our scene partners both through listening *and* adding when it's our turn.

This rings true beyond our current (at the time of writing) pandemic-stricken times in which racial injustice begs our attention. Before "Black Lives Matter" or "Me Too" were a part of the social parlance, and in a future when new social movements and slogans arise--there will be a need for leaders to ask brave questions and *yes, and* in a meaningful, sincere way. There will be a need for leaders to do more than keep up with the current culture trends and use the correct buzzwords.

Yes, and is about so much more than keeping up with the Joneses of human resources policy and culture strategy. A sincere *yes, and* is about something deeper. And so are you, or you wouldn't be reading this.

WHAT IS THE DEEPER *YES, AND*?

Through the lens of mindful improv, *yes, and* can be understood as requiring equal parts *humility and courage*.

Really, that's what we're doing here. Yes= humility, And = courage. Effective improvising on and off stage requires us to maintain both things in equal measure. If we lean too heavily on one side, we're either copping out of the scene or bulldozing our scene partner.

We need humility to believe that the scene partners around us are worth collaborating with, even when we've seen them get it wrong before. Humility helps us believe that really great ideas can come from unexpected places and situations. Humility reminds us to trust that things can go differently than we expect and still be wonderful.

In improv, saying "yes" is about the humility to lean in to other people's contributions and treasure them for what they are and for all that they can become.

But it's of course not enough to always sit back and watch others contribute to the scene. At some point, we must summon the courage to add something of our own. This is what it is to *and*.

And is critical for everyone in the scene. Without *and*, you might as well be in the audience. *And* helps new team members gain a sense of belonging, and it's the "how" of collaboration: folks must contribute. But *and*-ing is especially a responsibility of leadership.

It's a leader's responsibility to *and* on the most tender and vulnerable pieces of culture, where the execution is just as important as the intention. Therefore, it behooves heart-centered, empathy driven leaders to learn how to *and* with mindful purpose.

In improv, "and" is not about strong arming your will into the scene. It's not about asserting yourself simply because you feel like it's your turn. It's especially not about proving to your team that you're a good leader.

In improv, "and" is about supporting your scene partner and contributing to what she or he is trying to build. In servant leadership, *and* is about sacrificial support of your team members after you have *yes'd*.

I've gotten really delicious notes from improv coaches in the past about the role of "and" having nothing to do with *obligation* and everything to do with JOY. Please take a moment to consider these implications. **Contribute out of joy, not out of obligation**. If this were the only thing I learned about life as an improviser, it would still have been a transformational experience.

BUT ANDREA: you just said that *and* is a critical responsibility of leadership?! How can something be a responsibility without being an obligation?

Thanks for asking. The answer is: *don't do shit until you're in alignment*. Like: zero. shits. We'll address alignment thoroughly (what it is, how to know if you're in alignment, and what you can do to get back into alignment quickly) in the next chapter.

For now, know that alignment helps you *and* at the height of your integrity. It's the difference between a leader who reacts rashly in the moment or a leader who responds in congruence with their values and good intentions. It will help to ask questions like these before adding to a scene:

Did I already do the "yes work?" Did I listen with humility?

Is my contribution supporting the foundation my scene partners have laid?

And a final question that requires special consideration:
Is my contribution needed/necessary?

As Charna Halpern, Kim Howard and Del Close note in their book *Truth in Comedy,* there is an art to noticing when you're not needed on stage. In fact, they go so far as to suggest that noticing when you're *not* needed is just as important as having a viable contribution when you *are* needed!

In my corporate work, I have seen this concept resonate with leaders who struggle with micromanaging or have trouble delegating. Sometimes leaders need to be reminded that it's safe for something to get done *differently* than they would do it; this realization helps them notice when they're not needed on stage.

A subtler component is noticing when you're in *proving* energy: the times when your focus shifts away from honoring yourself and your scene partner and onto what others may be thinking and your need to prove your own belonging or worthiness of their love, respect or appreciation. This is something my girl Brené Brown brought to my attention the first time I read *The Gifts of Imperfection,* and I could fill about 17 books with the moments of personal growth I've experienced because of this simple understanding: proving is not an authentic or helpful motivation for action.

This is vastly applicable in the context of mindful improv. You cannot ever offer a sincere *"and"* from a place of proving energy.

Improv was immersion therapy for me as I worked through my need to prove stuff to people. I rarely (if ever) assume others have accepted me as part of the group: as a Christian, as a feminist, as a special needs mom, or even as a survivor of sexual assault. My assumption is that I have too many faith questions, too little knowledge of feminist heroes, too much perceived normalcy as a parent and too many years since my traumatic experience for the group to agree that I belong there. I have *frequently* found myself in proving energy in those environments, which is exhausting and has often resulted in my avoidance of the very supports that I needed.

Improv helped me with this. No other environment had ever felt so foreign and yet so familiar at the same time. I had practice at managing proving energy in almost every show; I learned from the low-stakes improv environment about the negative consequences of proving on relationships, collaboration and feelings of belonging.

For example, the temptation to slip into proving energy is especially strong on nights when you know certain people are in the audience. It's not just celebrities, casting directors, or producers you want to impress, by the way. Seeing my *mom* in the audience for the first time sent me through waves of proving energy!

Please don't let her feel embarrassed for me! Please don't let her think I'm wasting my adulthood. Please, please, gods of comedy, let tonight go well!

The frustrating reality is the harder you try to prove that you're funny, that you deserve to be on the team, that you stand out in your field or whatever else... the more you'll make awkward, selfish decisions that will embarrass you upon further reflection. These decisions will ultimately take you *further* away from your end goals.

Proving is not what inspires effective collaboration, or meaningful adjustments to company policy...or really anything else.

We've established that "proving" is when our behavior is motivated by our desire for validation and the need to feel "worthy" *in front of our scene partners*. In addition to proving energy, *performance energy* can also derail your brave conversations about the things that matter in your office. Another lesson from Brené[6].

"Performing" is when we seek validation and feelings of worthiness from people *not* directly involved in the scene...AKA: the audience. Very often, this happens at the expense of our scene partners.

But let's back up for a second. Because in order for you to fully understand this concept, I need to explain more about *where* improv shows happen. Improv doesn't happen in a traditional type of theater where there are costumes and props and scenery and precise lighting and sound cues, etc. (Well, not unless you're a cast member on *Who's Line Is It Anyway*. **smile emoji**)

At the average comedy venue, improv happens in a "black box theater." Imagine four walls, a simple stage set with a few chairs and several rows of audience seating. That's it.

This simplicity serves a purpose! It invites the audience to imagine with us. It invites the audience to *believe* the world we're creating by removing any distractions, or any extra stuff that could convince the audience they need visual aids in order to believe us. The simplicity helps the audience agree with the mayhem and whimsy happening onstage; it invites creativity on your part and on ours.

So if one person says "It looks like these murders were committed by a homicidal chicken," as in Colin's example from the foreword, the audience is willing to go into that strangeness with us.

---

[6] Seriously: if you haven't already gotten your hands on a copy of *The Gifts of Imperfection*, do yourself a favor and Amazon Prime that shit right now.

"Oh dear!" they say to themselves, "A man has been murdered! I wonder why a *chicken* would do such a thing!"

New improvisers don't trust this magic yet.

They panic when a non-reality-based offering comes from their scene partner. To keep from seeming foolish, they may sell out their scene partners and say something like "Umm, are you okay? It sounds like you were having a strange dream where chickens are capable of wielding a weapon."

Depending on the set up and the delivery, the audience may laugh. This may feel rewarding, but remember:

The primary goal of improv is to support your scene partner; not to make your audience laugh. *It's not okay to sell out your scene partner for the sake of the audience.*

It may seem counterintuitive, but it's true. We as performers are each other's first priority in improv, not the people in the audience.

The invitation of improv is to trust that this process of listening and building, listening and building, listening and building (*yes, and; yes, and; yes, and*) will not only result in something of comedic value, but that the result will be *so much more satisfying* than the cheap audience laughs garnered by selling each other out (and the audience may not laugh!). As a performer, you (and the audience) will enjoy the experience more when the players on stage work together to build the show.

Here's the rub: you perform in a comedy theater for drunk strangers who have paid money for you to make them laugh. The temptation is to just *give the people what they want* at all costs.

Off stage, the "drunk strangers" are your clients, or your investors, or your viewers, or whoever it is that's observing your "scene work." It's good to care about their experience. But bringing mindful improv into your work means that you provide the desired client experience by prioritizing your *people*, not your clients. You do this by working to do the best possible job you can at the humility- and-courage dance.

If that sounds implausible, get ready to plaus[7]. Prioritizing team members over clients is the central concept of Vineet Nayar's book *Employees First, Customers Second*. In it, Nayar writes:

"Through a combination of engaged employees and accountable management, a company can create extraordinary value for itself, its customer and the individuals involved in both companies. Thus, when a company puts its employees first, the customer actually does ultimately come first and gains the greatest benefit, but in a far more transformative way than through traditional "customer care" programs and the like."

Employees First, Customers Second is decisively fantastic. Without realizing it, Nayar has written a book that beautifully exemplifies what mindful improv looks like in a purposeful leadership space.

Can you trust that the result you most desire can be realized-- and to an even greater and more satisfying degree--by putting your scene partners first and the audience second? In a world preoccupied with compound annual growth rate and the proverbial *bottom line*, can you make it your dominant intention to support your scene partner (team members)?

---

[7] Interpret this how you like. It definitely means either *believe me* or stand up and start clapping... but I'll let you pick.

THE "I'VE GOT YOUR BACK" RITUAL

The improv philosophy you've just read is more than a "nice idea" to improvisers. Holding true to these ideologies is the only way we are able to succeed on stage! Before every show, improvisers remind each other that supporting one another is their dominant intention.

In the green room--basically a holding area back stage where performers wait before it's their turn to go onstage--we touch the shoulder of every person on the team and say "I've got your back."

We do this because our temptation is *to* get in our heads and make the show about the audience and our *need* for them to love us. But if the goal is to build something we can be proud of, our most important job is to honor our scene partner; to look for ways to be supportive instead of looking for ways to judge their decisions and determine we're the smartest, funniest, most skilled improviser in the room.

If the "I've got your back" ritual existed without the ideology, it wouldn't mean that much. It would be an empty, meaningless gesture like when baseball players hit each other's butts. (That's a thing, right? It seems like that's a thing. Maybe this is a key part of baseball culture?) But if the value/idea existed, and there *weren't* rituals to re-attach us to that guiding principle at critical moments, we could lose touch with those ideas and principles.

Properly-timed rituals can help bring us back to who we really are. Right before a show, adrenaline is pumping and the temptation to bail on the patience-required work of collaboration is highest. That's the perfect time to remember what we're really doing here.

Rituals can help intangible things (like servant leadership) manifest into tangible things (like making a team member feel heard and supported) when we need it the most. That's why I do this activity with every single client; each staff training begins with every person in the room making eye contact with each of their team members and telling them "I've got your back."

What could this mean for your team? What could this look like in your real life? What are the moments when you're most tempted to give in to people pleasing/audience pleasing instead of having the backs of your scene partners? Having the temptation doesn't make you a weak leader--it makes you a human person who's become enamored with the audience. Implementing a personal or shared ritual can help you get out ahead of that tendency.

"NO" IS NATURAL

It's inevitable that new improvisers say "No" a thousand times to their scene partners' initiations before they finally learn to say *yes*. We are conditioned to provide counter points and to play "Devil's Advocate."

Drs. William R. Miller and Stephen Rollnick explain this in their work on *motivational interviewing,* another tool I use extensively with clients. Motivational Interviewing is a method developed by Miller and Rollnick for supporting someone's behavior change efforts by asking them purposeful questions to help them tap into their own inner wisdom and motivation.

I learned about (and fell in love with!) motivational interviewing when I worked with veterans who were trying to quit smoking. I was one of the people working on a research study that was trying to identify what actually helps people quit smoking effectively. Because of this job, I had the opportunity to learn MI from some of the best trainers in the country. When I revisited those training notes years later, I was struck by how the fundamental principles of motivational interviewing fit with the mindful improv values of honoring your scene partner, listening with curiosity ,and receiving everything as a gift.

I also loved the way MI encourages you to change how you understand and respond to resistance and nay saying.

What Drs. Miller and Rollnick have found as they've trained thousands of doctors, nurses, and social workers hoping to successfully coach patients through addiction recovery is that the presence of "no," or initial resistance, *does not indicate a lack of willingness or ability to move forward with change.* Instead, they teach MI facilitators to expect and roll with this initial resistance.

Because of the human inclination to say "no" first, one of the worst ways to encourage behavior modification is to point out all the reasons why change is important, and then to suggest all the methods for how it can happen[8]. Instead, Miller and Rollnick teach MI facilitators the E-P-E method: elicit, provide, elicit. You elicit reasons for change and possible solutions *from the client,* and then provide resources or ideas in accordance with their offering. If that's not *yes and,* I don't know what is.

---

[8] Miller, W. R., & Rollnick, S. (1991). *Motivational interviewing: Preparing people for change.* New York: Guilford Press. Miller, W. R., Zweben, A., DiClemente, C. C., & Rychtarik, R. G. (1992). *Motivational Enhancement Therapy manual: A clinical research guide for therapists treating individuals with alcohol abuse and dependence.* Rockville, MD: National Institute on Alcohol Abuse and Alcoholism. Rollnick, S., Heather, N., & Bell, A. (1992). *Negotiating behavior change in medical settings: The development of brief motivational interviewing.* Journal of Mental Health, 1, 25-37.

Here is where I'm actively stopping myself from writing the rest of this book on Motivational Interviewing and it's intrinsic and powerful overlap with Mindful Improv. I *will* write that book in the future, and it will be called *MIAMI: Mindful Improv And Motivational Interviewing*. And the book launch will be in Miami! And we will do beach yoga! And there will be annual retreats!

But for now, when you start to build a *yes, and* culture at your office by having brave conversations and get met with resistance, I encourage you to not give up. It's human nature to say *no* first, even if the change being initiated is ultimately what we want and what meets our needs best.

CHAPTER SUMMARY

The deeper *yes, and* that heart-centered leaders long to provide in response to racism, sexism, able-ism, or any other kind of ism is not offered through any one finite response, whether that be a training, a new policy, or adjustments to recruitment and hiring. The deeper, healing, sincere, and productive response is owning the "courage and humility dance" EVERY DAY.

That's why forgiveness work is so critical. You cannot consistently hold up your end of the tango without forgiveness. Without forgiveness, your efforts to respond in critical, vulnerable moments will be rooted in proving (sounds like: "Please don't think I'm a racist!"), or denial (sounds like: "We're a family--we don't have those problems here!"), or any number of other not-the-best-you-can-do fallbacks to assuage your comfort (looks like: seeking approval or applause from your echo chamber, avoiding the issue, etc.).

So now you know the basis of mindful scene work. That is to say: you know what's really happening inside *yes, and,* AND how to be intentional about listening and contributing accordingly. BUT you can't really put this into practice without knowing when to do what.

Is it my turn to listen, or my turn to add something? Am I being silent in a way that is damaging to the people counting on me to speak up, or am I speaking when I should listen? Am I noticing when I'm not needed on stage versus when my support would be beneficial?

You will receive the answers to those questions when you're in alignment. Alignment is where we're headed in the next chapter.

CHAPTER 3: HEALING YOUR SOUL SPINE

We can make ourselves miserable, or we can make ourselves strong. The amount of effort is the same.

~ Pema Chödrön

I once visited a chiropractor because of chronic "smush pain that feels like everything fell out of the sandwich." (Where are my *New Girl* fans?) I had been nearly bedridden for three days because of awful neck pain, and for weeks thereafter I was limited in my range of motion. I was having trouble sleeping and was a real *peach* to be around, generally speaking. At least I *think* that was the word my husband Kyle was using…

When I arrived at the chiropractor, the doctor told me we were just taking x-rays to determine my treatment plan at that visit. No adjustment. No actual pain relief. He pulled down a chart and explained the spinal regions, and I swiftly kicked him in the nether regions. (Just kidding.)

But his stupid chart did nothing whatsoever to help me, so I left with a very clear understanding that I have the crooked back of your average Disney witch, but without any relief from the pain.

It hurts when your back is out of alignment. It also hurts when your *soul* is out of alignment.

To help you avoid the turdish, nonhelpful behavior of the chiropractor, this chapter will explore three things: the *logistics* of being in alignment as I've come to understand it, how to tell when you're not aligned, and what you can DO to regain this sense of inner wellbeing before responding or reacting to *anything*.

This chapter is pain relief for your soul spine.

WHAT IT MEANS TO BE IN ALIGNMENT

Alignment is a balanced state of mind, where you've gotten back in touch with your values and true identity. Alignment is when you're at peace, and you're making decisions with purpose and intention. When people say they need to "clear their head," what they are really saying is "I need to get back into alignment."

Your spine is in alignment when your cervical, thoracic and lumbar vertebrae are *lined up* so they can move and function properly. (Fine, I learned something from his stupid chart.) Your *soul* is in alignment when trust in yourself, your scene partners, and the unfolding nature of life are lined up so you can move and function in a way that represents your highest self.

When I first started improvising, I got horribly nervous before every show. On nights when I was performing, I couldn't eat for the *entire day*. Even without eating, I often got an upset stomach before my team was brought on stage.

The theater where I performed had two very small bathrooms with and very thin walls...you could hear everything. The looks of disgust mingled with pity on the faces of audience members in line after me are seared into my memory forever.

One such evening, I was especially in my head, having noticed that some of my day job coworkers in the audience. I was pacing in the green room, feeling very nervous and most certainly slipping into *proving* energy.

My coach noticed this and offered the best possible words of encouragement: "Just be playful!" he said. "You can't break it if you stay in *the spirit of play.*"

My load lightened immediately. *Just be playful. I don't have to prove anything to anyone.*

I thought about this every time I felt nervous before a show. *It's not my job to be hilarious. It's just my job to stay in the playful spirit of collaboration.*

A spirit of playfulness is what enables balanced, beautiful collaboration. Playfulness is not about proving or perfecting or forcing my agenda on anyone else. Playfulness in improv is how we hold the scene lightly, knowing that a career in comedy won't be made or broken in a single night--and a comedy career definitely *won't* be created by choking the life out of every scene with desperation and attention seeking.

The longer I practiced playful mindset before a show, the more I realized that it felt familiar. A playful mindset wasn't really about being *playful*; it was about being *peaceful.* It was about re-establishing trust that I and my scene partners could handle whatever was about to happen.

This was *alignment.*

The more I worked this over in my mind, the more I became curious about how to understand this playful, aligned mindset in a practical sense. I wanted to understand what was happening so I could choose to do it proactively.

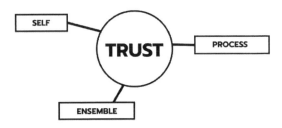

Thus this diagram was born, which I call The Trust Tripod.

I call what the Trust Tripod represents *the spirit of play* when I'm on stage, but I call it being *in full alignment* in my off-stage scene work (AKA: life).

Having a visual understanding of what "inner peace" actually *is* has helped me create so much more of it in my life. And improv is an immersive experience at regaining this mindset! So many things can go "wrong." So many things can trigger a shame spiral, or push me into proving or performing territory... and the spirit of play gently pulls me back to where the fun is. Or better said, where the *magic is*.

The spirit of play is where unthinkably magnificent works of collaboration can be built. Some of my most joyful adulthood memories are from the intense, vulnerable experience of building something in front of an audience from a place of 100% trust.

I hope you can imagine the deliciousness of applying this mindset in life! The payoffs aren't as immediate as they are on stage, but they're also *way more important*. Instead of audience laughter indicating that you're on the right track, here's what the spirit of playfulness looks like in real life: a moment of reconciliation between team members at work, an amazing opportunity for which someone else opened the door, or even a joyful breakthrough after a tough conversation with your daughter.

Imagining those successes for you is the soul equivalent of a homemade cinnamon roll on Christmas morning. Mmmmm. I want these moments for both of us, like, so bad.

UNDERSTANDING THE COMPONENTS

To help you recognize which leg of the tripod is out of alignment, let's take a closer look at each component: yourself, the ensemble, and the process. These are not listed in order of importance; rather, we need *equal faith* in each of these three things:

1. **Self**: We must believe and have total faith in ourselves. We must believe that we are capable of offering valid and meaningful contributions, and that we are allowed to take up our space and participate in the story. This leg of the tripod can also be understood as *worthiness*, a word I've noodled with for a long time. To help you identify if and when you're out of alignment with *yourself,* here are some examples of what "out of alignment with my own worthiness" looks like for me:

- Struggling to say out loud what I want or need
- Isolating myself, especially from people who (I feel) are better at whatever I'm feeling insecure about
- Procrastinating on telling people how I really feel
- Projecting my fears and feelings onto other people
- Gossiping or participating in character assassination to make myself feel better

- Filling my head with fear-based news, movies, articles to justify the "it's hopeless" narrative I'm nursing
- Hiding from confrontation to avoid making others uncomfortable

These behaviors are rooted in *limiting beliefs*, or beliefs that are both untrue and unhelpful for my goals in life. In the case of the behaviors listed above, the limiting beliefs are: other people's needs and feelings are more important than mine, speaking my truth is dangerous for my relationships, and my insecurities or weaknesses dictate my future.

When I isolate, gossip, project, and procrastinate on speaking my truth, the story in my head sounds like this:

Everyone else is dealing with this (inappropriate boss, bully at work, difficult client or other negative situation). Why can't I deal with it? Why can't I push through this like everyone else? I'm too sensitive. I'm not tough. I'm not a 'real' adult.

or

Sharing my perspective will just make waves; it's safer to keep quiet.

or

In the grand scheme of the world's problems, how big of a dent can one person really make? It's hopeless. Why do I even bother?

or

Because of what I've done, I don't deserve _____.

Listen up! The story you're telling yourself about your value, worthiness, and your *creative impulses* is directly affecting your ability to connect with other people and represent your ideas in the best light. *It's also affecting the scale of impact you can make while you're on this planet.*

You've heard Henry Ford's quote "Whether you think you can, or you think you can't -- you're right." I used to feel so discouraged by that quote, because in my heart of hearts, I didn't believe I could accomplish my goals. I didn't even believe I had permission to have my goals in the first place. The good news is, you can re-wire your brain to *think you can!* For me, it started with re-wiring my brain to *notice* self-doubt and negative self-talk. You can't interrupt what you don't notice, so it's very important to learn how to become aware of this happening in your brain. The more I became aware, and inside of that awareness chose to be curious instead of judgmental, the more I found forgiveness opportunities *everywhere* that helped me rewire my brain and start believing I am capable of creating and worthy of having of good things in my life.

In doing this work, I began to notice that when I'm in alignment, I feel pulled or *drawn* into the scene. I feel *joyfully compelled* to participate. When I'm out of alignment, I feel *obligated,* or sometimes *afraid* of, participation. Sometimes my participation is about *proving* or *belonging*. Esther Hicks says that pursuing goals when we're out of alignment is like "pushing a rope," which is an analogy that hits home for me.

Fear and obligation will not take us closer to our goals and intentions. I call action that gets us closer to what we truly want a *creative impulse,* and a true creative impulse is born from *delight* and *the pleasure of collaboration itself*. Read that again. A true creative impulse brings you joy in and of itself.

Those moments of joy are only possible when we're in alignment with our own value and worthiness. It's possible to experience fleeting moments of joy without being in alignment, but the journey of your life doesn't have to feel like a treacherous, booby-trapped labyrinth of misery! We can find joy and peace in our lives, even amidst circumstances that are stressful or troublesome. I have found this to be true as an entrepreneur, as a foster parent and as a small business owner sticking it out through a global pandemic.

We do this by getting into alignment, and then taking action...not taking action because we're hoping to find joy in other people's applause, respect, or admiration. Other people can't love you into alignment. You have to love yourself there, my friend.

Tapping into the truth of your own worthiness is especially important ahead of confrontation. Confrontation provides the potential for growth and relationship building; we can choke out that potential with frantic, aggressive behavior that doesn't represent the whole of who we are.

Sometimes we act frantic and aggressive because we fear the other person and what they represent. Other times, our lack of alignment is caused by something very tangible: like being tired, hungry or overwhelmed.

When we have unmet needs, we cannot be our best selves; nor can we access the clarity we need to collaborate at the caliber of our intention. This is basic self-care. As parents, leaders, pastors and business owners, we hear about *self-care* all the time. Yet we still:

- Participate in office cultures that prize the "hamster wheel/grindstone/burning the candle at both ends" mentality
- Allow ourselves to be baited into arguments about stuff we care about when we're exhausted, hungry, or sad
- Make important decisions when we're motivated by fear, anger, or resentment, instead of when we feel pulled by enthusiasm, love, and optimism.

When we do these things, we slowly erode our emotional reserve and our connection to *who we really are*. So let's stop doing that!

Regardless of whether our misalignment is caused by a physiological problem (hunger or exhaustion, for example) or limiting beliefs around worthiness, it is critical that we rehabilitate the "self" leg of the tripod before we take action. This takes some time; but *you are worthy* of taking time to get re-aligned. Re-alignment time may not even take as long as you think! For example: in the journey to adopt our children from foster care, I often had to testify in front of their biological family in court. Fifteen seconds of deep breathing before taking the stand helped me regain alignment.

2. **Ensemble**: In improv, there's a lot that must be in place for you to believe it's safe to trust the people around you...especially after you've observed their shortcomings. Here are some of my favorite lessons learned on stage:

–> *My scene partners are more than their shortcomings.* You've heard me say this in several different ways already, but it's worth repeating. We all need grace for the journey. Each of us is more than the worst thing we say, do or believe.

–> *There's not always a stated invitation, or a clear opportunity to get out on stage and add my idea.* But the lack of an invitation does not mean there's a lack of openness to my input. More often than not, your ideas are more welcome than you realize; it's up to you not to let the chaos on stage convince you of a story that no one cares what you think.

–> *If we wait for perfect scene partners in order to offer up our most vulnerable, creative ideas… we'll be waiting a long time.* The scene partners you have are the scene partners you need. Maybe you read that sentenced and thought "No way! If I could only get rid of so-and-so, *then* things would run much more smoothly!" Here's a piece of clarity and an action item: if you don't trust your scene partner, they shouldn't be your scene partner; but if you *do* trust them, give them the opportunity to show you what they can do, and what you can do together. It is damaging to culture and it's damaging to your relationship with your own inner voice to stay in perpetual indecision in these situations.

As we say in improv FOLLOW THE FEAR! Fire them if you need to. Leave if you need to. Take a big risk and get coffee with them if you need to. Ask brave questions, reassign projects, go axe throwing or sit with a mediator. This is improv and there is *a broad and vast horizon* of possible next steps.

Maybe you feel tangled up about whether you don't *trust* someone or you just don't *like* or *understand* them. The former is about *inner wisdom* and the latter could be about bias or could simply mean you're encountering a new template for how people can move through this Earth. I've been there! Several years ago, I was collaborating with someone who was an expert in her field, and in an openly polyamorous relationship. After she shared this with me, I thought I didn't *trust* her. Then I realized that polyamorous…ity (?) is just so, so new to me. It's extremely different than how I roll in my

Mennonite world, and even though it had nothing to do with me, it felt shocking and even worrisome. When I realized the root of my funky feelings, I was able to quell my fears about working with her: I didn't mistrust her, this was just new and it made me uncomfortable. Uncomfortable isn't bad. You have permission to be uncomfortable – you're a human being. But don't limit yourself to where you're comfortable. It's so, so boring.

"Am I hearing inner wisdom, or am I hearing inner bias?"

This is an *excellent*, world-peace-building, massively self-aware question to be asking. This is why it matters to have a diversity of trusted voices as mentors, advisors and fellow leaders. It's also why learning to parse out your inner voice from the cacophony noise coming from the least aligned corners of our polarized echo chambers is so important. Folks will have an opinion no matter what decision you make, so the best you can do is make a choice that honors your true character, your big vision and the other people involved.

–> *Your scene partner can't surprise you if you don't give them the opportunity.* If you get so committed to a story you've been telling yourself about who someone is, you may not be able to see the person instead of the story. People say "You can't judge a book by the cover." But I say, "You can't judge a scene partner by the book you made up in your head."

It may feel like a lot of work to commit to the scene partners in your life... and it is! Marriage is work, group dynamic is work, co-founder relationships are work, maintaining ties with relatives across state lines is work... there's no getting around the work. Relationships worth having need tending.

But really leaning into the idea that *it's safe to trust your scene partners* is a critical part of collaborating well with them. Most of us can admit that our "personal lives" effect our "professional lives" from time to time (spoiler alert: it's just ONE life we're living, so that makes sense). Because of this, it's no surprise that expanding this work to your family and social circle scene partners, thereby improving your relationships with them, will also improve your effectiveness and impactfulness as a leader. You will micromanage less. You will overwork yourself less. You will notice when you're not needed in a process, conversation, or even confrontation; you absenting yourself when necessary will serve the highest good of everyone involved.

Trusting your scene partners is a freedom-enhancing leadership skill. Trust that it's safe to do your part, not everyone's part. It's not your job to be the one building every time. Isn't that freeing?

3. **Process**: I once had an improv teacher tell me that a successful improv scene requires that you "bring a brick, not a cathedral." What he meant was, "Andrea, stop trying to control the entire scene!!" (As an improviser, I've had to work harder at the *humility* piece than the *courage* piece of the yes, and equation.)

More broadly applied, "bring a brick, not a cathedral" means that you bring one piece of the scene, and offer it to the ensemble or your scene partner *as a gift*. Then you *listen* as the others add their bricks. Piece by piece, you build whatever it's going to be together.

That means even if we're the first person to talk, on stage or in a critical boardroom meeting, it's still our responsibility to "yes, and" with our scene partners. There's no getting around it! We *yes, and* our way through the entire scene by listening for the new and current offerings of our scene partners and then building on top of that.

I find this incredibly freeing.

"Bring a brick, not a cathedral" means that, in order to initiate the scene, you don't *need* to know 11 steps down the road how something will play out. You can just get started! The outcome isn't your job. *Participation is your job.* The weight of the entire show is *not* resting squarely on your shoulders, and your shoulders alone.

Sometimes leaders maintain an outsized sense of control, and consequently, responsibility. Yes, you have decision making authority; but the deeper truth is that *no one knows what the future holds.* I've witnessed the heartache of leaders forced to make layoffs in 2020. I've cried alongside leaders carrying the heavy weight of uncertainty as the entire world waited to see what SARS-COV-2 had in store for us. As a leader, you are not orchestrating outcomes by yourself: it's you AND your ensemble, which includes the unseen forces of the universe. I'm very happy to take a deep dive into "the unseen forces of the universe" over mojitos, but what I'm getting at is that *it's safe to move boldly into the unknown.*

To "trust the process" is to understand that when you move in alignment, you'll always have what you need. Your job is to observe with an open and ever-curious mind and ask: "what is my next brick?" Leading with *yes, and* is embracing the ping pong inside of the Chess game. Allow me to explain.

Leaders think multiple plays in advance – like Chess. It's *great* to be prepared and to leverage your strategy-creating brain… until there's a global pandemic, and all you can do is be agile amidst ever-changing circumstances. Now you're playing ping pong, just trying to hit the ball as it flies at you from different directions. You put something out there, new information comes, and it's time to pivot. Ping pong is a game of immediate response.

Strong improvisation requires both: patience and agility. It's like a hammer: one tool with two sides that do opposite things. The way to tell which side to use - the bangy part or the claw part – is to ask what the scene needs right now. Do I need to add a nail or remove a nail? If we're adding a nail, we need the bangy part. Please enjoy the mental image of someone trying to hit a nail with the claw side of the hammer: *that shit would be unsuccessful.*

All day long, bangy part for adding nails. For life and leadership, the two sides of your "improv hammer" are patience and hustle. If you're anything like me, you'd pick the fast pace of hustle every time.... But that's exhausting and lonely and unattainable.

Some of my favorite business advice for knowing which side of the "improv hammer" to use in real life comes from Gary Vaynerchuck. He says "Macro patience, micro speed." I have circled back to this many times as I build my cathedral alongside the unseen forces of the universe. For the big picture, long-game things that are most important to me: I choose to be patient. For example, this book project commenced in June of 2019. In entrepreneur years, I've been working on it for several millennia. (Evidently in publishing years this is an unsurprising timeline.) At every moment when I was ready to jump ahead despite questionable publishing terms or ill-advised timing or poorly-defined audience, seasoned authors and people with more experience than me pep-talked me on patience. *Take your time. Do it right. Let the path unfold naturally.*

For the day to day: speed! Don't overthink your social content. Don't procrastinate on asking brave questions, or taking action on the things you're confident must be done. Is there an event you'd really like to speak at? Pitch yourself! See someone at a networking event that you'd like to meet? Go introduce yourself! (This is how I met one of my favorite, long-time mentors.)

Sometimes we hesitate to lay our next brick because we're waiting for the perfect strategy to emerge. But for all you know, whatever you're about to lay down *is* the perfect opening that will invite one of your scene partners to respond. Your scene partner's response can provide clarity and the path forward you've been working so hard to find on your own.

Life is improv. Improv is unfolding moment by moment. It is safe to lay your brick and trust that process of unfolding.

ALIGNED CULTURE

I am convinced of several things in life. One, as afore mentioned, is that Amy Grant is the greatest living musician of all time. Another is that the culture on your team and at your company is forged in confrontation.

Culture is not determined by donuts or posters or ping pong tables in the office... although those things are great for Instagram and recruitment purposes. Culture is about confrontation. Have a group of people who avoid saying what needs to be said, OR bulldoze each other fueled by hot-lava rage? *All of the donuts in America cannot compensate for that problem.*

Understanding what it is to be in alignment, how to get back into alignment on demand, and the importance of not doing anything for *any reason* until you're in alignment: that knowledge will help you build culture through confrontation.

Think of the bricklaying vs. cathedral-building analogy. What happens in most confrontations --which sabotages us before we even get to the conversation itself--is that *we bring a cathedral to a bricklaying party.*

On stage, "bringing a cathedral" might look like this: an improviser on the sidelines plans out the *entire scene* before she has even entered.

"I'm going to be a doctor who's completely hypochondriacal, and it's my first brigade with Doctors Without Borders. And I'm slowly falling in love with the doctor stationed here in Calcutta. And then later, we could meet the ghost of Mother Teresa, and then Kevin could do a callback to his Gandhi character, only this time he would be a ghost, too and really – this would tie the whole show together so nicely. Maybe we could have a group game with ghosts of all the world's wise teachers together, only they can't agree on how Heaven should work. We could make them really passive aggressive since they all pretty much practiced nonviolence –how funny! I wonder if I can pull off the ghost of Menno Simons?[9]"

There is no possible way the improviser was listening to what was happening on stage while she thought of all that. She should go write a sketch, or even a screen play for that matter!

The reason this approach is problematic (aside from the not-listening issue) is that you can only initiate so much at a time... so if you've already crafted how you want a scene to go, you'll continue not listening *while you're on stage* this time, because you're so busy trying to orchestrate the scene according to plan. When things shift away from your vision (which they

---

[9] My editor assures me that non-Mennonites do not know who Menno Simons is. He is the 16th century Catholic priest turned anabaptist rebel for whom the "Mennonite" faith tradition is named.

absolutely will as your scene partners add their own bricks), you'll hurt their feelings and distract from what is being built by strong-arming the scene back to your original vision instead of embracing what it has become!

I know this from experience. I'm a top notch cathedral-bringer who's had to work extra hard at leaving those Type A planning behaviors behind when I step out on stage!

In life, bringing a cathedral to a confrontation might sound like what I've done in the past with my husband:

I can't believe Kyle didn't offer to pick up our son Cooper from daycare. He knows I have slides to prepare, videos to edit and work to delegate before my trip tomorrow. Doesn't Kyle realize I've been the one to pick Cooper up every day for the past two weeks? This OBVIOUSLY means:

…He doesn't take my business seriously. Last month wasn't my most impressive month financially… of course he expects me to do this; he expects me to do <u>something</u> *to contribute to our relationship!*

…Or what if he's not as bonded with Cooper as I am? I've heard that bonding is even hard for biological dads, so it's probably even harder for adoptive dads. What if Kyle and Cooper never have a meaningful relationship?

…I'm not selfish for wanting to work and be a mom. Why doesn't he realize it makes the most sense to favor the schedule of the entrepreneur with unlimited income potential? If he can't see that, it's because he doesn't believe I can do this… and if he doesn't believe I can do this, maybe we won't make it.

A few years ago, the simplest co-parenting snafu could send me spiraling into "Kyle doesn't love me," "Kyle doesn't love our kids," or "We are probably going to get divorced."

I've heard from enough people to know that I'm hardly alone, and hardly in the minority for spiraling *hard* when it comes to something I'm sensitive about.

Our favorite cathedrals to bring into confrontation are the *cathedrals of insecurity*. What we are most sensitive about has a tendency to easily find us when we're out of alignment.

We have imagined the intricate details of these cathedrals thousands of times, and we know their architecture well. These are the cathedrals for which we reach first, and we can find evidence of their structural integrity any time we want.

Before I understood alignment and proactive forgiveness, I was the jedi master of making *everything* point to my cathedrals of insecurity.

But even now that I teach these things for a living, I'm not immune to my own Insecurity Cathedrals. If I'm falling off of my self-care game, and the conditions are ripe for my insecurities--for example, a client I was excited about backs down at the last minute at the same time that I have to go bathing suit shopping after weeks of wayward gym attendance --I'll still hear echoes from the darkest corners of my heart:

- You guys got married too young – your husband feels the perfect amount of stuck and comfortable to ever tell you… but you know he doesn't *really* love you.
- Think about all the embarrassing things you've said when you were depressed… You're a *hot mess* who gets less hot with each passing year.

- The bond with adopted children isn't as strong as the bond with biological children. You'll never have the closeness other people have with their kids.
- Ha! *Everyone* has a book to write. Why bother? You are insignificant.

Friends – I don't know what you hear from the darkest corners of your heart when you're feeling the most vulnerable, but here's what I do know: YOU'RE HEARING LIES.

They *are* lies. But they're also lanterns, casting their clarifying light on our unprocessed stories and pointing us in the direction of our growth opportunities. When we get into the proactive forgiveness process, you'll learn how to use these cathedrals of insecurity to identify exactly where forgiveness work can provide you the most freedom and clarity.

For now, understand that when you're out of alignment, your cathedrals are just lies. They only become lanterns when you're *in alignment*. If you carry your cathedrals into an important confrontation or a sensitive situation while they are still lies, your cathedrals will poison your experience by affecting what you say and how you say it.

Your cathedral will keep you from learning from confrontation. Pay attention to your self-talk ahead of confrontation. You may be saying things like:

This person thinks _____ about me.

or

This is the kind of person who _____.

If either of those thoughts don't line up with your new understanding that you are worthy, that it's safe to trust your scene partner and it's safe to trust the process of unfolding… that's how you know you're building a cathedral.

Get yourself back into alignment and then bookmark whatever lies came up for further investigation later. That's what we'll do in the proactive forgiveness process.

The Inherited Narrative Cathedral

There's a second kind of cathedral worth discussing, and that is the *Inherited Narrative Cathedral.* An inherited narrative cathedral is the story we've been told a thousand times about our lot in life, or what kind of person someone else is, based on the trauma and experiences of the ones who came before us.

Please hear this: there is a difference between receiving someone's *story* and receiving someone's *cathedral of insecurity.*

Receiving someone's cathedral means we are receiving their limiting beliefs about what is possible. We are taking on their shame, resentment and fear. We are taking on their biases and emotional limitations. Receiving someone's *story* is listening wholeheartedly to someone's experiences, feelings and needs. Receiving someone's story is about growth and deepening our understanding of what has transpired in the past, so we can make more informed movements in the future.

It is important to distinguish these two things. Inherited narrative cathedrals are often presented with stories, but it is possible to parse the two apart. The cathedrals are the limiting beliefs inside the stories.

Inherited narrative cathedrals are especially hard to buck, because they come with generations worth of *evidence* virtually *proving* their validity.

When the generations before us shared their experiences of trauma, exclusion, marginalization and oppression with us--that was their truth! That was their story and their experience.

Their reason for sharing it with us was likely threefold:

- To lighten the load of carrying all of that hurt on their own,
- To protect us from entering a potentially dangerous situation with naïveté, and
- To inspire us to work toward something more just, equitable, and beautiful

It's important to analyze the stories that have been passed down to us through the lens of alignment. Yes, And doesn't require us to say "no" to history or truth. In fact, doing so couldn't be more *out of alignment*. Saying "no" to a story that makes us sad or uncomfortable is a fear-based response. We are afraid of what will happen when we acknowledge the story, which is backwards; the only thing to fear is what will happen if we *don't* acknowledge it.

Yes, And isn't about ignoring the past. Yes, And is about *not being limited* by the past. It's about embracing what has come before AND adding something new on top of that.

It is possible to receive someone's stories without receiving the limiting beliefs attached to them. We can do this by listening with empathy, and by allowing ourselves to take the actions that will result in a more positive future. We can listen and act from *joy!*

Cultivating change doesn't have to be miserable, soul-sucking work. When we spend our time imagining the world we want instead of focusing all of our attention on what we *don't want,* and when we remind ourselves how many amazing scene partners we have by our side, we can learn from our ancestors without letting their pain push us into hopelessness.

That's not what our ancestors wanted for us anyway! They want freedom, growth, and joy for us! They want to see us take our place in the story of restoration being written all around us, for the big and small things that need restoring.

Our ancestors want their stories to be paving stones to help us on our journey, not weights holding us back. It's important not to forget history. And it's important to remember that we can still build something beautiful.

To have a meaningful impact in the world—which is the intention of every heart-centered leader I know--we must embrace positive change, trust the scene partners around us, and do the vulnerable work of collaborating with imperfect people.

That is why we must keep our stories and those of our scene partners and surrender the cathedrals. We must be aligned for this work.

HEARING YOUR INNER VOICE

The more I incorporate the concept of *alignment* in my corporate and community work--the more I teach about the ways our beliefs and feelings are shaping our decisions and behavior--the more people tell me how difficult it is to achieve alignment because it requires you to listen to your inner voice.

You can't get into alignment if you can't detect the nudge toward one thought path versus another. *You just have to practice!*

Don't know how to hear your inner voice? Start by interrupting negative self-talk. If you constantly tell someone they're stupid, ugly, irresponsible, fat, etc., *that person is not going to readily offer advice or guidance!* It's the same with your own inner voice. If you're constantly judging, shaming, and berating yourself, why would *yourself* want to talk to you?

If you beat yourself up and then wonder why you can't hear the clear voice of guidance calling you along your path, it's because *your voice is scared of you!* Be kinder to yourself, and you'll find it easier and easier to hear your inner voice, get back into alignment, and find the clarity you need.

A second strategy to access your inner voice is to reframe what you may call *reading the room*. Accept that most people are *not* picking up on your thoughts, motivations, and desires... they're making up stories based on *their* deepest fears and insecurities. Their stories don't have anything to do with you.

I often remind my clients that until they've mastered the art of getting and staying in alignment, they are *never* reading the room; instead, they're reading and projecting their fear narratives.

Have you ever heard the theory that *you* are every character in your dreams? It's the same for "day" dreams too! Day dreaming here means the time you spend determining what someone *really* meant by their ambiguous/possibly hurtful words or imagining arguments that haven't happened yet: not the time you spend wondering how much work is involved with boat ownership. When you're imagining that other people are thinking negative things about you, that's your inner voice saying "I'm afraid of something! I'm insecure! I need to be reassured." Notice this voice. Then, start asking yourself: "Why am I afraid? Why am I insecure?" As you explore with sincere curiosity, you'll identify opportunities for healing and forgiveness.

You *do* have an ever-present inner guidance system that's beckoning beyond the noise of your daily life. It's always inviting you closer and closer to *who you really are.* It's up to you to practice listening for that voice.

Third, practice reflecting and listening for your inner voice when you're in neutral emotional territory. If you're only reflecting when you're worried or something is royally pissing you off, hearing your inner voice will be much harder. Practice listening to your inner voice in the morning, just for a few minutes. It's a simple a practice as this: "How am I feeing right now? Hmmm… I wonder why?"

Listening for your inner voice is a helpful daily practice. Remember our trusty three-legged tripod? If you get stuck in your efforts to reinstate one of the legs of the tripod (faith in self, faith in others, or faith in the process), I hope these mantras will be helpful for you as they have been for me:

- It is safe to be imperfect. I am enough.
- My scene partner is more than this one thing.
- Worthiness is not determined by a single moment.
- It is safe to do my part, and not everyone's part.
- I am capable. I am courageous. I am willing. I am worthy. *Capable, courageous, willing, worthy.*

HELPFUL MINDFULNESS PRACTICES

Mindfulness is what helps us notice, in any given moment, whether all three legs of the tripod are balanced. If not, the best thing to do is identify which leg is out of whack. Here is a mindfulness exercise that helps me do this proactively, so I can choose my alignment at will instead of being stuck waiting for happiness or peace to find me.

I've learned that how we feel determines what we think and how we react: if we're feeling lousy, we think negative thoughts, and then we feel worse. If you're not in alignment, you'll be stuck in a cycle of not-in-alignment- thoughts, feelings, and behaviors--unless you proactively interrupt that process. The following exercise will help you break the cycle:

MINDFULNESS EXERCISE
FOR GETTING BACK INTO ALIGNMENT

When you're feeling a negative emotion of any kind (regret, worry, resentment, or just general negativity) rather than letting it fester--or leaning into the lie that those feelings are a part of your identity--try this:

1) Say to yourself "Negativity is *not* natural for me, but it might be here to help me see something. What is this calling my attention to?"

2) Which leg(s) of the tripod is the negativity knocking out of balance? Am I negative about myself, someone else, or the process of waiting for things to happen organically?

3) What happened that caused me to forget my worthiness, someone else's, or the safety of patience?

4) Reground in your *deep truth* using mantras, affirmations, prayer, meditation, or EFT tapping.

It's worth noting that finding alignment when you need it isn't the same as *processing your story* via the deeper work of proactive forgiveness. But this exercise is a great place to start, and then put a pin it for later. For example, if you were given difficult feedback at work and haven't had time to fully process that feedback...if you start to spiral and feel certain that you're turning out just like your father...this exercise can help you regain your inner peace. But it's important to put a pin in the "Am I just like my faither?" question for deeper reflection later.

Your brain has carved out thought habits and patterns around certain subjects, so you're very used to feeling a certain way-- and therefore thinking and behaving a certain way—when you dwell on sensitive subjects. After you do your processing, alignment can help you retrain your brain to connect with feelings of worthiness, trust, and optimism when those sensitive subjects come up. This alignment exercise is powerful, but it's not a workaround from truly processing your painful stories. The process I'll share with you later in this book can be very helpful for doing that deeper work, but I also hope you feel the freedom you need to seek help from a therapist if you need it. I am eternally grateful to the many therapists I've worked with in my life.

FINAL THOUGHTS ON ALIGNMENT

Living in alignment is how we feel joy, freedom, and growth. What I've come to believe and teach is that negative feelings of any kind are showing us that one of the legs of the tripod is misaligned. The most important thing you can do is figure out which leg is out of whack, and then re-anchor yourself in your deep truth. Your deep truth is the truth you know even when you don't feel it.

When I was in the second grade, my family had just moved to Nashville, TN from Canton, OH. I was having trouble adjusting to our new normal – I missed my friends and family in Ohio, and shortly after we arrived, we found out that the job promised to my mom had fallen through leaving us in an uncertain and unstable situation. I still hadn't fully healed from the traumatic experience of sexual assault, and I would occasionally spiral into a darkness beyond what I felt I could control. With much compassion and empathy, my dad used to encourage me to "Separate what I feel from what I know." I think that's really good advice: it's helped me feel grounded and taken me out of thought spirals. I've had big feelings ever since I was a kid, so this thought exercise has been useful for me many times over.

As an adult, I've come to a new understanding of the relationship between feelings and truth. Feelings aren't the *opposite* of truth. Feelings are pointing at truth we've yet to discover.

Exploring our feelings is useful because the process often leads us right to our highest ROI forgiveness opportunities. The Mindful Exercise for Getting Back Into Alignment in this chapter sets you up perfectly for the forgiveness work you'll learn about in the next chapter.

Committing to this work (alignment and forgiveness first) will enhance many areas of your life, not least of which is confrontation. **How you engage confrontation determines how much belonging we feel in our relationships**, and informs our sense of identity and engagement with the people around us.

What this means practically: Instead of rehearsing an argument in your head ahead of a confrontation...if you are in alignment, you'll lay the groundwork for a more effective conversation.

After all, life is *improv* not a scripted play! As much fun as it is to imagine Uncle Cranky Pants saying hurtful things and Witty Wonder Woman having the perfect comeback that leaves a room full of gobsmacked family members in an awestruck and grateful silence…that imagination session is helping you write a script. And a script won't help you in real life, around the Thanksgiving dinner table. At least, not for long.

Your script will be useless as soon as your scene partner surprises you with information you weren't expecting. We know this, but so often we exhaust our pre-confrontation energies imagining the other person's rebuttals. We justify our expectation of the worst outcome by re-living our worst experiences with that person.

Spend your time getting into alignment and planning how you'll *stay* in alignment when you get to the conversation. *You'll have the words that you need when you're in alignment.* That is true for improv on stage and off.

CHAPTER SUMMARY

Getting into alignment is your first and most important job as a leader. It's also a deeply fulfilling way to live your life. If you're in alignment, you'll be the person you intend to be more often. Being in alignment means that you have equal faith in:

- Yourself
- Your scene partner(s)/ AKA: The Ensemble
- The process of letting things unfold naturally

We're tempted to weigh down confrontations with our unexamined stories and deeply-rooted insecurities rather than sticking to the knowable facts. This is called bringing a cathedral instead of a brick. It's safe to enter the unknown with your simple brick, and trust your scene partners (including the unseen forces) as well as the gentle process of unfolding. Together, you can build something amazing.

Getting into alignment requires diligent practice and listening to the guidance of your inner voice. You can practice doing that by:

- Interrupting negative self-talk
- Reframing the experience of *reading the room*
- Working through the Mindful Exercise for Getting Back Into Alignment when you're in *neutral emotional territory*

CHAPTER 4: FREEDOM THROUGH FORGIVENESS

"To forgive is to set a prisoner free and discover
that prisoner was you."
~ Lewis B. Smedes

"The weak can never forgive.
Forgiveness is the attribute of the strong."
~ Mahatma Gandhi

Let's continue on our journey toward a new understanding of forgiveness as an empowering, healing act of self-discovery and self-actualization. Forgiveness is the single most important soft skill a leader could ever master.

Forgiveness gets a bad rap. Many people believe that until you can recall the most painful chapters of your story without feeling rage, despair, shame, resentment, etc...then forgiveness must not have happened.

I challenge that notion. I'm not interested in training my brain *not* to be outraged by injustice. As a foster/adoptive parent who has been through trauma therapy with my (then four-year-old) daughter, I can vouch for the fact that some things should *always be infuriating*.

But I'm also not interested in giving away all my mental real estate to the worst aspects of my story or anyone else's. Constant focus on what's *awful* does nothing to create more of what's beautiful in the world.

What *does* help me work as an agent of good in the world--and in my own life--is being free of the limiting beliefs that pull me into shame, pessimism, and suspicion of others. That's what this chapter is about, because that's what *forgiveness* is about.

To me, forgiveness is when my hurt is no longer writing my story.

I know this 'f' word is kerfuffling. I want to be explicit about what forgiveness is and isn't.

What Forgiveness Is NOT:

- The process by which we absolve someone of a wrongdoing.
- The ability to remember an injustice without anger or sadness.
- Interchangeable with the words "That's okay."
- The peaceful destination you reach after years of unpacking your hurt.
- A moral obligation, or the means to becoming a *better person*

Often as children, we're taught that forgiveness is what happens once you've "worked it out with your sister." You return each other's Barbies, and then Mom watches intently as you offer apologies through clenched teeth.

In these exchanges, we're inadvertently taught that forgiveness is the absence of anger--that it's the service rendered in exchange for an apology. Forgiveness is treated as some kind of binding agreement to "move on."

Here's what I know: forgiveness is about *freedom*, not absolution. Forgiveness has nothing to do with whether or not you're a good person, but it has everything to do with whether or not you're a *free* person.

So if we let go of the old tropes about forgiveness... what *is* it, then?

Forgiveness IS:

- The prerequisite for effective confrontation
- An internal process that can be tracked, outlined, and observed
- How we identify limiting beliefs which stem from past pain, and choose beliefs that serve our purposes
- A process that's never "finished;" it's a process that cycles in perpetuity
- A spiritual invitation to become a *freer person*

Since it's an internal process, forgiveness has nothing to do with anyone else. It does not require an apology, it does not require a "forgivable" offense (by society's standards), and it does not require you to change how you feel about what happened. **Forgiveness is not about looking to the past and making peace with injustice... it's about looking to the future and seeing the possibility for good things to happen, despite the past.**

If you're wondering *how* forgiveness accomplishes this, the answer is in the logistics. When we forgive, we are identifying *limiting beliefs* and replacing them with beliefs that serve our purposes well.

When we understand forgiveness this way, pain, worry, and other negative feelings are very helpful because they point us in the direction of healing. We can view them as problems or as helpful guides leading us to what we truly desire: love, belonging, hope, joy, etc. A negative feeling is tied to a memory, or a person with whom we have unfinished business, or a situation that has not been fully resolved; therefore, this negative feeling is still limiting our view of what's possible.

Mark Twain has a quote that exemplifies perfectly how limiting beliefs work:

"If a cat sits on a hot stove, that cat won't sit on a hot stove again. That cat won't sit on a cold stove either. That cat just don't like stoves."

In this analogy, getting burned is the traumatic/painful experience. The limiting belief is that "stoves aren't safe." It shows up in the cat's life through his avoidance of stoves.

Is the cat justified in that behavior? Sure! Why not? Who's to say if anyone else's trauma-related behavior is justified, so long as it's not harming anyone else?

> Sometimes painful things can teach us lessons we didn't think we needed to know.
> ~ Amy Poehler

It's really easy to get hung up on the *justification factor* when we're dealing with limiting beliefs related to our most sensitive traumatic experiences.

As a survivor of childhood sexual trauma, I know this well, and I sincerely empathize with those in my trainings and workshops who struggle to embrace the concept of forgiving their perpetrators or others involved in their victimization.

But here's the ish: my lack of forgiveness of the person who assaulted me and the limiting beliefs I held as a result of that situation—those were holding me back from fully connecting with my husband and children.

I'm not interested in holding onto my resentments because other people believe they're justified. There are plenty of things other people may never call me out on, but those things are holding me back nonetheless.

When we define our beliefs and behaviors at *justified* instead of *courageous*, we lay the groundwork for our life experiences at *survivable* instead of *wonderful*. ...and friends, I don't know about you, but I want *wonderful!*

If you're tempted to hang on to certain resentments or wounds because "No one could ever judge you given the gravity of what happened," I implore you to choose forgiveness anyway. Not because the perpetrator of your pain deserves it, because YOU deserve it. Your ability to engage and connect with the people around you depends on it.

Your ability to be the leader you *mean* to be--not just the leader you can manage to be while carrying so much extra weight-- also depends on it. Fortunately, you don't have to wait until your feeling forgivingish. You can proactively choose *at a time when you're in alignment* to do this work.

THE PROACTIVE FORGIVENESS PROCESS

There are two simple processes I want to offer for beginning proactive forgiveness work. These two processes have helped me find peace quickly if I'm not in a moment where I can go all the way into the rabbit hole.

First, a process for the most common catalyst of forgiveness work: intrusive memories of something hurtful. Let say you're lying awake at night replaying an embarrassing or infuriating situation. No matter how hard you try, thoughts of what happened, how you responded, and what you wish you would have done or said differently keep returning to you. I've been there.

Perhaps in the past you would have lain there replaying the events over and over, hoping to arrive at some helpful conclusion--usually, what you believe you can do differently in the future to prevent similar humiliation, hurt, or disappointment.

Alternatively, you might seek relief from these intrusive thoughts by getting out of bed and turning on the TV or opening the pantry.

I've been there, also. Ask me how many boxes of girl scout cookies I ate at midnight in the when we were trying to adopt our children from foster care.

But rather than continue to distract yourself from these invasive thoughts, or ignoring and redirecting the thoughts[10], try this instead. Ask yourself what limiting beliefs were planted in your mind and heart because of that situation.

For me, the limiting beliefs often start with:

- "That's the kind of person who..."
- "That person thinks _____ about me."

---

[10] These are both completely legitimate coping skills for some points on the journey, but for the purposes of learning this skill, let's say you're ready to address the situation head on.

- Now _____ [piece of my future success, growth and/or joy] is impeded in some way.

Sometimes forgiveness work starts with a clear memory of pain, and from there we can choose to ask: "What limiting beliefs did I internalize through that experience?" Other times, we can initiate forgiveness work through the recognition of a limiting belief. In that case we ask, "When did I start believing this?" in order to conjure the memory of a specific situation. It works in both directions.

It takes focus and intentional curiosity to draw the connection between these thoughts and events. The very act of getting quiet to do this work can be soothing in and of itself. But beyond the initial, momentary relief of pain, identifying the limiting beliefs gives birth to so much future freedom and groundedness.

Now for the second process, which I use when a negative feeling finds me and I'm having trouble shaking it off. This process helps me hold space for my negative feelings and reinterpret them as helpful *forgiveness guides* rather than intrusive pests. My friend Erin, a trauma therapist and fellow improviser, calls this process "acknowledging and allowing." I call it: super helpful.

Perhaps in the past when you've had a negative feeling you couldn't shake, you've decided to ignore it and push through. Instead, try asking: *why is it here?* "Hello jealousy. What's up, self -righteousness?! I see you sadness. Thanks for showing up. Why are you visiting me right now? What are you here to teach me?"

Once again, we will go on the hunt for limiting beliefs.

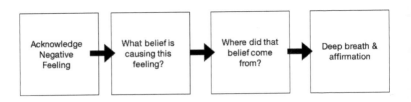

Sometimes I refer to this simple thought exercise as "naming and releasing." There is power and freedom in identifying the cause of something (read emphasis on the word *cause*).

The bad feeling or the negative belief isn't *part of you*. It is separate from you. Even if it's really, really "bad." Even if it's dark or hateful. That's not YOU. That's a separate thing: a feeling, a belief, a thought.

And it was caused by something. It's not an immovable, *true* thing you have to carry around forever. It's not an indivisible part of your identity. It's about something old, and you get to decide if you carry it into your future or not.

Naming and releasing can be very simple in practice, but it can be so powerful: especially when we allow ourselves to say each piece out loud. As Mister Rogers says, what is mentionable is manageable. We cause so much shame and heartache by deciding that certain things are not mentionable, either because we think they're too big or too small.

Your feelings are valid. You can trust them as forgiveness guides. Mention them: even just to yourself.

Here's an example of how I used this simplified process to begin finding freedom and relief for the "heading home for the holidays" *dread* I experienced year after year when we lived in Pittsburgh. As it turned out, my dread unearthed a critical forgiveness opportunity.

THE SNOWBOARD SHAMING OF 2001

In the winter of 2000 headed into 2001, I was learning to snowboard. I was very bad at it, and lost interest quickly. So Ellen, when you read this story and have me on the show: you don't need to send a snowboard to my house. But I appreciate the instinct, you giant hearted sunbeam of a person.

All of my friends were in the ski club at my school, and I wanted to be too. My sweet mom took extra shifts and worked overtime to make that happen for me. I was *delighted* when she told me I would be able to join. We scoured local thrift shops for a heavy-duty, water resistant coat to keep me warm on the slopes of Boston Mills/Brandywine Ski Resort. We found a silver and orange one from some brand I was excited about back then. Never mind the faint staining or the slight gap between the end of the sleeves and my gloves. "No one will notice!" I pleaded.

I felt such pride slip knotting my lift pass into the zipper of that coat. It was one of the first times I felt like I "fit in" with the other students at the small private school I attended. Many families there were quite wealthy (at least that was my perception).

My family received a generous scholarship and financial aid package to attend. Even so, I knew my parents felt immense pressure to make the payments; they were working multiple jobs and struggling to make ends meet. As the oldest (and nosiest) child, I wasn't unaware of the money-related tears, arguments, and fear in our house.

But none of that weighed on me as I boarded the ski lift with my classmates and awaited my first lesson.

Several weeks in, I noticed that the boys paid extra attention to girls on snowboards, and I wanted in on that action. To be clear, I wanted to be noticed and given the opportunity to say "I'm sorry--I'm only dating Jesus right now." Yep. I've got an entire Rebecca St. James *Wait for Me Journal* full of entries backing this up.

One November afternoon, my sisters and I were at a cousin's house looking at catalogues and planning our Christmas wish lists.

"What are you asking for?" my cousin asked.

Knowing the expense, I nervously announced that I wanted a *snowboard*. I showed him the one I wanted in the catalogue. It was light blue and had snowflakes on the bottom. Without missing a beat, he replied "Me too! But... your family probably can't afford it."

His words hit me like a fist in the throat. It felt like someone had taken a melon baller and scooped out all my dignity. I felt hallow, heartbroken, and humiliated.

I don't remember what I said next, but I do remember crying in the bathroom … and the long, uncomfortable wait for my mom to pick us up.

What made his words feel so heavy wasn't just that they were true. I already knew most of the people around us had more money and stability than we did; but I hadn't realized until that moment that anyone *else* noticed or cared enough to make such a blatant observation.

I felt trivialized. I felt like he was looking down on my parents, who are the bravest, kindest, hardest working people I know.

Before long, the rage and shame turned into suspicion and fear... *Why does he know that my family "probably can't afford it."? How many people in my life know that?*

I started making up a story that his parents must have told him things my parents had shared in confidence about our financial situation. I pictured his family sitting around their dinner table in their perfectly tidy, chandelier-clad dining room full of fancy expensive dishes, discussing my family's financial woes. This (likely fictional) mental image was hurtful and humiliating.

It wasn't long before the fear-narrative in my head extended into other social circles as well. My cousin went to the same small private school, sans-scholarship, and we were being raised in the same church. If he knew... what if they *all* knew? The thought of people in my church, my neighborhood and my extended family judging or pitying my family slowly eroded the safety I once felt to be myself in those spaces.

I started feeling unworthy around my friends and family, and in time I started feeling unworthy around anyone who had more money than my family. I felt such shame anytime the subject of money came up.

Around that time, *Legally Blonde* was taking junior high sleepovers by storm. I saw it countless times and even bought the soundtrack, sneaky style, at the mall when my parents weren't looking... truly an act of rebellion in a family where the music was closely monitored for non-Billy Graham-approved themes. They were very fine with my unceasing love of Amy Grant.

The protagonist of this movie, Elle Woods, was wealthy, beautiful, well-liked and motivated to do great things. She epitomized everything I wanted to be. I tried to memorize and emulate everything about her. As I write this, I am white knuckling my way through cringe-worthy memories of pencil-shaped, newly-pubescent Andrea doing *the bend and snap* in public.

For three years, I died my hair blonde, spent over an hour before school on hair and makeup, and changed my speech patterns and mannerisms to match those of Elle Woods.

It. Was. Exhausting. (As faking it *always* is.)

This nonsensical behavior carried through my sophomore year of high school, until some changes in my family necessitated a change in schools. Although I fought it tooth and nail, I got a desperately needed clean slate, and the chance to be myself again.

At my new school, I ceased the phony, superficial weirdness, but the limiting beliefs and feelings of unworthiness around money followed me into adulthood.

As we got older, the snowboard shamer cousin and I gravitated toward notably contrasting political persuasions, which only deepened the suspicion, anxiety and fear I felt around him. Our family circles remained strongly connected, and I became the queen of argument rehearsal before holidays when I knew I would see him.

About five years after Kyle and I were married, I was feeling acute distress as we drove from Pittsburgh to Canton, Ohio for Thanksgiving. I had recently left my highest paying job ever to build *something* improv-focused. I didn't really know what yet. But it was exciting, and I was proud of myself and *happy*. Despite my joyful adventure, we were barely scraping by in those days, and I was just plain *dreading* the experience of seeing the snowboard shamer and facing the judgement and ridicule I was sure lay in store.

I had completely demonized him, and had allowed this person to become an ever-present, invisible judge in my life. With every career move and financial decision, he was in the back of my mind criticizing, outperforming, and reminding me of what *probably wasn't possible.*

Me allowing him to become a fictional caricature of himself didn't happen overnight. This thought pattern had become so normal to me that I didn't even realize how frequently I was thinking of and resenting my cousin. I only realized I was doing this because of some critical *naming and releasing* work. Here's what that looked like:

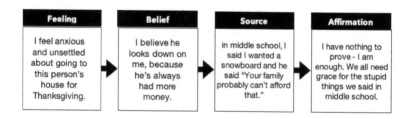

Feeling	Belief	Source	Affirmation
I feel anxious and unsettled about going to this person's house for Thanksgiving.	I believe he looks down on me, because he's always had more money.	In middle school, I said I wanted a snowboard and he said "Your family probably can't afford that."	I have nothing to prove - I am enough. We all need grace for the stupid things we said in middle school.

It took years for me to do the full deep dive, but using the simple process, I felt a wave of relief (and genuine enthusiasm about pie, which is all any of us should be feeling on the way home for Thanksgiving).

If the "full shebang" forgiveness process is the knee surgery you've got scheduled in two months, this process is the Tylenol and ice pack that will help you out until then.

The simple realization that I was thinking of my cousin so often, that I had demonized him, and that I was rehearsing arguments that hadn't happened, helped me be present in the moment and connect with the joy that was right there available to me.

My time reflecting in this different and purposeful way also yielded a powerful realization: *there is a difference between running away from something and running toward something.*

I had spent *so much time* trying to prove my worth to him and running away from shame, financial insecurity, and the embarrassing memories of the person I was in high school, that I hadn't really identified what I was running toward. I didn't have a *true north*. Besides, trying to prove your worth to people who aren't evaluating it is completely pointless and unnecessary.

Investing myself in that journey of discovery—"What am I running *toward*?"--has lead to many wonderful relationships and so much personal growth. It's amazing what even a few moments of focused thought can reveal when our dominant intention is to heal.

THE STAGES OF FORGIVENESS

Often when we think about restoring a relationship--or trying again with something important after we've been hurt--we are able to identify that we're "just not there yet." But we've got no answer to the more important question:
Where are you, then?

I want to help you answer that question via the Stages of Forgiveness chart below. This chart is a visual to help you understand what you need emotionally, and what you can do in order to keep healing.

I developed the Stages of Forgiveness process informed by my work as a smoking cessation interventionist in my social worker days. (I am truly still a social worker... just in a completely different setting than I ever imagined back when I was getting my Social Work degree! My career has taking several surprising left turns, but the spirit of social work has remained intact throughout.) During that time, I was trained in the *Trans-Theoretical Model* (TTM) and Prochaska and DiClemente's *Stages of Change*[11]. You can find more information about their work and this evidence-based coaching/support method at www.andbeyondimprov.com/bookresources.

In full integrity, the *The Stages of Forgiveness* is something I created based on observing and analyzing my own experiences and those of clients and peers. This is not a scientific tool; but I've found it to be incredibly helpful in my own life, and as a tool for my clients who are working to grow into stronger leaders, entrepreneurs, pastors, and parents by proactively working through their forgiveness opportunities.

I hope it's as meaningful for you as it has been for us.

---

[11] James Prochaska and Carlo DiClemente are American professors of psychology who's developed The Transtheoretical Model of Behavior Change in the 1980's. Their work has deeply informed the way those in the helping professions understand the mechanics of behavior change, and therefore help people follow through on positive behavior modification.

THE STAGES OF FORGIVENESS:

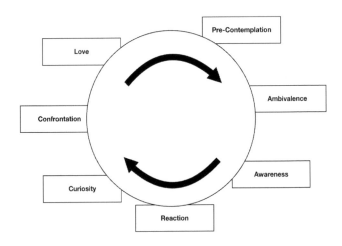

Each stage in the process plays a part in the healing journey. All that matters is your *intention to heal* and your *proactive effort*. There's no competition, no race to be the fastest healer ever. I ask that you read these stages for the sake of understanding and give yourself permission to be honest about which stage you're in.

To help you understand these stages, I'll provide a brief description of each one; then I'll share a story from my life to provide an example of what these stages can look like in the real world. Incidentally, the stories I'll share form the foundation of why I'm so passionate about equipping leaders to be who they mean to be, more consistently. I'll tell you about how I learned that extremely toxic cultures can easily be created at the hands of very knowledgeable, very well-intentioned leaders. I'll tell you how I learned that without heart work, your brain work doesn't matter.

Stage 1: Pre-Contemplation

Description: In this stage, we are not consciously aware of the ways in which our unprocessed pain and trauma are affecting our daily decision making, attitudes, and beliefs. We may remember an event that caused shame, but we've disassociated from it and haven't yet mined what it has to teach us.

How to Identify Pre-Contemplation: We feel lonely and isolated despite having opportunities for connection. In this stage, we often make decisions based on internal beliefs about *possibility* rather than considering whether or not we *desire,* or could benefit, from something.

For example, "I cannot part ways with my cofounder: we're in too deep!" instead of "Since I know parting ways with my cofounder is what I truly desire, let me think about how to do that honorably."

Stage 2: Ambivalence

Description: In this stage, we acknowledge the effects of the shaming event on our current life--to an extent. But the emotional work required in order to allow the memory to resurface for healthy processing feels too overwhelming. Maintaining status quo feels the safest.

How to Identify Ambivalence: We feel shame or resentment towards others, *especially other people involved in the incident.* We may also feel anger, resentment, or jealousy towards a.) people with a similar story or background who have achieved more than we have, or b.) people connected to the situation who (seem to be) further along the forgiveness journey.

Stage 3: Awareness

Description: In this stage, we realize that the costs of maintaining the status quo outweigh the costs of processing our pain in order to change our behavior, attitudes, and thought patterns. We are fully aware of the stakes of continuing to allow our unprocessed hurt to steer the ship.

How to Identify Awareness: You suddenly see the impact of your story on the people around you. It's become more painful to maintain the status quo than to venture deeper into your story and fully acknowledge/reckon with your pain.

Stage 4: Reaction

Description: Now that we recognize the cost of maintaining the status quo, we react to that awareness. Perhaps we become inundated with thoughts of missed opportunities, missed connections, time wasted, and/or concern for the consequences to ourselves and the people we care about.

How to Identify Reaction: In this stage, our sympathetic nervous systems may be activated via the fight or flight response. We may become prickly and defensive, or feel the need to hide from the weight of our feelings, we may need to cry... or some combination of all of these!

Shame and catastrophiz-ing are hallmarks of the Reaction Stage. We may feel many things at the same time and struggle to figure out what to do next.

Stage 5: Curiosity

Description: In this stage, we consider the painful event and its aftereffects with *curiosity instead of certainty or judgement.* This allows us to begin the important work of considering other perspectives; more importantly, this is where we do the work of noticing the limiting beliefs we have internalized from the situation. As new moments of Awareness arise, we're able to avoid shame and blame by getting curious about WHY something happened, where it came from, and what it was about.

How to Identify Curiosity: We ask questions instead of making internal judgment statements. *We choose self-compassion and grace* as we begin to explore the situation and our feelings about it from a new perspective. One question may be, "What did this situation cause me to believe was true about myself or anyone else?" Curiosity allows pain and other negative emotion to become *forgiveness guides.*

Curiosity allows you to consider that perhaps your nightmares and the flashbacks and intrusive thoughts aren't here to burden you. Perhaps they're here to release you. What if they're pointing at where freedom is waiting? What if your hurt is asking for your attention so you can resolve your limiting beliefs and find a joy you didn't know was possible?

Stage 6: Confrontation

Description: In this stage, we are confronting the narrative we've told ourselves about this painful event. This is an *internal confrontation,* not external. Meaning, you are confronting *yourself* about the narrative; it is <u>not necessary</u> to confront anyone else in order to successfully confront the narrative.

How to Identify Confrontation: We're assigning responsibility appropriately, taking ownership of the role we played in the event and/or it's aftereffects, and assigning responsibility elsewhere for the things that are *not ours to carry.*

The inability to assign responsibility appropriately is a strong indication that there's more exploring to do in the curiosity stage. If you are a survivor of sexual trauma or any other kind of traumatic assault and you have difficulty assigning responsibility, you could benefit from outside help as from a therapist.

It's not your fault. You have nothing to own here. Difficulty assigning responsibility is common for traumatic assault survivors… you are 0% responsible.

For the many, many other situations needing proactive forgiveness work, taking ownership of your role in the situation is critical. It's not about blame or fault. Truly. Taking ownership is about *agency.*

You can be and do and have anything you'd like for the next chapters of your life, but only if you understand fully the amount of control you have over what happens in your life. If you assign all the responsibility to other people, you're saying "I have no control." This leads to feelings of powerlessness, apathy, and a victim mindset.

Conversely, taking on ALL responsibility, to the point where you feel buried in shame, is also debilitating. You are not responsible for other people's behavior, so don't shame yourself into oblivion by taking on more than your share of responsibility in a situation.

This is a balancing act. This is also *yes, and.* This is courage and humility work in action. The deep truth is: *life is improv.* We've built the past scenes alongside our scene partners, and our own contributions have shaped our stories and experiences just as much as anyone else's contributions.

Internal confrontation is not about blame, it's about regaining your creative control.

Stage 7: Love

Description: Love is what we all want. We want to love ourselves; we want the love of those around us; we want to love the present moment. *We want to love the way ALL parts of our story have equipped us perfectly for the life we desire to lead.* <u>Love is the ultimate mindset for cultivating beautiful things.</u>

How to Identify Love: In this stage, we are able to identify and release the limiting beliefs stemming from the painful event and attach ourselves fully to a narrative of agency.

IDENTIFYING FORGIVENESS IN THE WILD

When Kyle and I had been married for three years, we hit a rough patch. As in, I didn't want to be alive anymore.

I was working two full time jobs: one that was providing our health insurance and putting Kyle back through college, the other a start-up I was getting off the ground with some friends. I often slept less than four hours, ate more fast food than I care to admit, and was not managing the stress of my two jobs well. Kyle had a part-time gig as a barista and was putting in the hours to earn his Computer Science degree. We rarely saw each other, and it was increasingly apparent that we were growing into very different people. This is not surprising since we were *children* when we got married, but still: it was hard and sad and lonely.

At my day job, my boss was a misery-inducing extension of Divine Light who often didn't remember to turn on her damn lantern. She had recently called me into her office and asked me to help her with an "important but not work related" project: finding evidence from a past research study that it's bad for everyone involved when People of Color move to the suburbs. I was horrified. "I'm not being 'a racist!'" she said with dramatic air quotes and a confident if condescending smile. "This is me looking out for everyone's best interests."

She was referring to a study called "Moving to Opportunity[12]" and--shockingly enough--the study findings absolutely, in no way shape or form, supported her initial claim or represented her initial characterization. When I said this to her, she said "Huh. The person who told me about this must have misremembered. No harm done!" Umm. *Much harm done.*

So that was my day job: catering to the bizarre and soul-destroying whims of my Principal Investigator, breathing through her accusations that there were hidden recording devices in our meeting rooms, listening to her make fun of people's accents, and observing in horror as she cornered research assistants to demand their input on whether or not her husband was gay. Like I said, she often forgot to turn on her lantern. When I approached HR with my concerns of her racism, bullying, and general toxic behavior, a steel-faced woman informed me that "She gets funded. So she stays."

---

[12] Tama Leventhal and Jeanne Brooks-Gunn, 2003: Moving to Opportunity: an Experimental Study of Neighborhood Effects on Mental Health. American Journal of Public Health 93, 1576_1582, https://doi.org/10.2105/AJPH.93.9.1576

Over in my start-up world, our advisory board had just told me I needed to fire one of our team members. Their reasons were legit, and I knew that in my heart, but she was my closest friend from college and someone I absolutely *did not* want to fire. I did it. It was horrible.

Not long after, my dark lantern boss gave me a "we're about to fire you" annual review. I had certainly become demotivated and short fused, and some of what she said about me was factual. (Some of it was about *a different person on the team* who was my same age, and she legit didn't know the difference, but that is neither here nor there.)

I felt trapped. I felt like a failure. My marriage was falling apart, I had lost my closest friend, and I was about to lose my job. I felt hopeless.

And that's when I decided to kill myself.

I had attempted suicide once in college, and the memory was so embarrassing--both because I had gotten that low emotionally *and* because I didn't know you couldn't kill yourself with a bottle of Tylenol--that I rarely thought or talked about it. I certainly hadn't considered the possibility that darkness like that could ever find me again. "It was a momentary lapse of judgement," I told my parents when they picked me up from the hospital.

Thanks to the ER doc's advice back in college, I now knew that "If you *really* want to kill yourself, you use something much stronger than Tylenol." Thanks, man. Note taken.

Let's look at what happened next through our stages of forgiveness. There are many subplots to this story that also make for awesome forgiveness opportunities. For the sake of clarity, I'll focus on my need to forgive Hannah--my boss who

was the primary antagonist of my nightmares at the time. Like...
I frequently woke up mid-nightmare dreaming that she was
stabbing me to death in the parking lot.

Pre-contemplation

Even though I held a degree and license in social
work, and even though I had advised many, many
people to seek help for their depression and to say
that word without feeling a sense of shame or failure...
I couldn't find that freedom for myself.

Not even with my *therapist* could I bring myself to be
honest about the depth of my darkness. I was honest
about the stressors in my life, and honest about my
past traumatic experiences... but anytime she asked
about suicidal ideation or "dark thoughts" as we
called them, I used shared jargon and my delightful
sense of humor to assuage her concerns.

I drove home from my terrible review with a familiar sense of
calm despair, having accepted suicide as the best course of
action. I imagined calling my mom, or one of my sisters for help,
but the thought of disappointing them or worrying them felt
too burdensome.

When I got home, Kyle was there. Class was cancelled and he
was home early. He asked why I was home at that time and I
could hardly look him in the eye and offer an honest answer.

I told him what happened at work, and that I was spiraling really
hard. He packed my stuff, loaded up the car and drove me to
Black Mountain, North Carolina. Some of our favorite friends
live there, and Kyle decided nothing could heal me faster than

mountains, chicken waffles and friendship. I mean: he wasn't wrong.

Ambivalence

We arrived at the Gribbenshire residence in the middle of the night and went straight to bed. Despite being exhausted from crying most of the drive, I was restless, waking frequently with chest pain, in a cold sweat and filled with dread. The thought of driving back to Pittsburgh and facing everything that awaited me was pushing me deeper into my despair. Quitting this job didn't feel like an option because of *income*. And health insurance. And Kyle's half-completed computer science degree.

The next morning, I could hear Kyle talking with our dear friend Sam. "I don't know what to do. It's so hard--I don't even know if she *wants* me to help her."

Awareness

In that moment I was overcome with feelings of being *loved and seen*. His words were so compassionate and sincere. I had been so busy blaming *him* for the coldness in our relationship, that I hadn't considered the possibility that my complete misery could be affecting him.

Reaction

My feeling of being loved was quickly interrupted by a high school shame story. Someone at a party had told a friend of mine that he didn't like me because "She makes her problems everyone else's problems." Maybe I did that in high school--I was more than a little dramatic and attention seeking. But here I was, an adult, on the brink of suicide worrying that it was happening again. (Forgiveness opportunity sub-plot!)

Andrea Wetherald, monopolizing everyone's time with her petty insignificant problems since 1998. Everyone hates their boss-- why can't I cope with it like everyone else? This is adulting--I can't believe I'm the wet rag everyone else needs to take care of.

Now that we were talking out loud about how close I had come to ending my life the day before, there was nowhere to hide. I was miserable at work, and my friends weren't going to drop it.

I spent the next two days hiking some of the most beautiful trails in the world with some of the most loving people I know and breathing the fresh air of *possibility*.

I remember seeing the ridge line from a particularly scenic overlook and thinking "Hannah doesn't own this. She's not in control of this. The world is bigger than her, and what if my joy and hope can be bigger than her, too?"

Curiosity

Kyle and I took many quiet car rides through the winding Blue Ridge Parkway, which yielded plenty of opportunities for me to wonder: is there a different, deeper truth in this?

I thought about Hannah's threat to "blacklist" me if I quit and make it so I "can never work in Pittsburgh again" (a threat she had made on several occasions to prevent staff from "defecting" from the study) ... was it possible that she couldn't really do that? If she did, was it possible I could just build a life somewhere else and be happy? Was it possible I would be better off just focusing on the start-up anyway? Would I be able to move things along faster without this constant weight around my neck?

After an intervention over chicken waffles in which my friends expressed their concern and their desire for me to quit my job,

I felt an emotional shift. Maybe adulting *isn't* just slogging through life, caught in a miserable situation. *Maybe adulting is being brave enough to believe something better could exist!*

On our drive back to our friends' house, we experienced the most delightful moment of Divine provision and grace. It is a treasured Ebenezer stone[13] moment for me.

Black bears. FOUR OF THEM. I love bears so much. It's a whole thing. I wanted to see them so badly, and had been assured throughout the trip that it was very unlikely.

It wasn't a good time of year.

Dryer weather was diminishing their food supply.

They mostly stay away from people.

So many friends have come to visit and left without seeing them.

Not me, man. I Law of Attraction-ed the actual shit out of this black bear sighting, and I didn't even know Law of Attraction was a thing back then.

The Mama bear crossed right in front of our stopped car walking on hind legs with her front arms outstretched in a show of power and intimidation. Then her *three* baby cubs

---

[13] The word Ebenezer means "stone of help." Growing up, I learned the ancient Hebrew story in which Samuel erects a stone in a battlefield after Divine intervention delivered his army from a dangerous run in with the Philistines. The stone became a reminder of God's provision and was a source of hope during times of struggle and hardship. This is what the words "Here I raise my Ebenezer, hither by they help I come" are referring to. Recording Ebenezer moments is something I do now for hope and resilience in my own *dark knights of the soul*.

scampered across the road in the worlds' cutest impromptu bear parade.

It was completely, positively AMAZING.

My lungs inflated with hope. I felt like a wilted flower coming back to life. We drove back to Pittsburgh and I quit my job. And Hannah blacklisted me in the places where she had influence. And I lived to tell the story.

As I unpacked that work experience and the many layers of emotional erosion I'd experienced during my time there, I ping ponged back and forth between *curiosity* and *reaction*. I did this for years. Forgiveness isn't a race, remember?

When the concepts of *limiting beliefs* and the stages of forgiveness emerged for me, I got proactive about working the steps on this story. My feeling of sharp defensiveness when I remembered the details of my terrible professional review guided me to my big freedom moment with Hannah.

I realized I was ducking responsibility. I *hadn't* been my best self in those days. I *hadn't* done my best caliber of work. I didn't deserve to be bullied and dealt with cruelly on so many occasions, but receiving critical feedback in some areas was very appropriate. I messed up. Everybody does. It is entirely possible to be a worthwhile person *and* be imperfect.

FREEDOM.

Accepting responsibility for my part in the situation, and re-rooting myself to the deep truth that *I am more than how I handled that*, gave me the emotional bandwidth to do

Confrontation

something that surprised me. For the first time, I could see Hannah the way Mama U sees her[14].

Before, my relationship with Hannah was clouded by fear and the imbalance of power between us. But from my new vantage point, I could see her clearly as a dearly loved human soul who was separated from her own worthiness.

For the first time, I remembered heartbreaking comments she had made about how her parents treated her. For the first time, I remembered when her mentor berated her in front of a room full of her staff saying "I never thought you have what it takes to get this done"...and she took that hit--from a *mentor*--without flinching.

I recalled the time she cornered a research assistant in the elevator and asked her point blank: "Do you think my husband (who also worked with us) is gay?" I felt *empathy* instead of outrage. She was lonely in her marriage. She wondered if she and her husband had grown into people who were too different to make it work. I know what that is.

> Love

For the first time, I fully appreciated the incredible opportunity I'd had to be trained in Motivational Interviewing by some of the finest MI instructors around the country: something Hannah made possible for me.

It was like a dam broke and grace came flooding in. I felt sincere sadness at the thought of this woman--a published author on the subjects of mindfulness and optimism--never allowing the

---

[14] Perhaps you know this entity as God or Source or Divine Love or Allah or Spirit or something else that's completely beautiful and perfect. I use many words for God Beyond The God I Name, but my sister and I are especially fond of *Mama U* where the U is short for universe.

goodness of her work to flow into her own life. I wondered if there were contexts where she was able to be a different, more aligned version of herself.

I sincerely hoped *good things* for her, and I sincerely believed *good things* were in store for me despite (and in part because of!) that season of my life.

Releasing the fire I felt in my soul toward this woman allowed me to regain a sense of self. I am compassionate. I am confident and brave. I am optimistic and playful. I am an extension of Divine Love.

There's also a strong possibility I wouldn't be doing my current work without A) everything I learned about neuroplasticity, the science of behavior change, and motivational interviewing while working for her, and B) the sharp contrast of feeling so much misery while working for someone who taught me what *mindfulness* is and had a huge poster of Buddha hanging in her office. That contrasting experience planted the seed for this work.

Fresh air in the soul. Thanks, forgiveness.

DANGER ZONES FOR GETTING STUCK:

While there is no rush to move from one stage to the next, there are three stages where it's easy to get *stuck:* ambivalence, curiosity, and reaction. (Note that stuck is not the same as *mindfully present.*)

Ambivalence. While every stage of forgiveness is the right stage if your intent is to do the work… the ambivalence stage has a tendency to shift our focus from "doing the work" to "staying comfortable."

Here's one way to identify if you're stuck in ambivalence: do an inventory of the times you've said "no" to new opportunities recently--big or small, work-related or personal. Not just a mental inventory – get out a pen and paper and make an actual list. Here's an example list of my no's from the last week:

- Virtual coffee/lunch catch up
- Taking on a pro bono client
- Letting the kids watch TV
- Hiring a certain publicity firm
- Exercising (glug. It's the truth, though.)
- Watching a comedian who's energy pulls me down
- Getting to sleep on time

Take a quick minute to really think about what all you've been asked or invited to do in the last two weeks; look through emails or texts if that's helpful. It could also be helpful to notice what asks or invitations you haven't responded to yet – are those pre-no's? Once you've got a short list, keep reading and reflect on your list with these questions in mind.

Are you shutting down opportunities for new things based on whether or not they're *feasible* rather than whether or not you *desire* the experiences? When presented with a new opportunity, ask yourself: "Would I like it if this thing happened? What if it *were possible* after all? What is the cost down the road if I miss out on it?"

Another great way to identify the ambivalence trap is *procrastination*. Are you dragging your feet on something important? Maybe you need to have a hard conversation with a colleague, ask for 360 feedback from your team…or maybe it's time to make a professional transition. Are you experiencing resistance?

If you find yourself stuck weighing pros and cons, people pleasing, or ducking feedback, these are great indicators that you're hiding from something. And that *something* holds wisdom, clarity, and freedom that are yours for the taking!

If you can approach the situation with curiosity, you'll see that the source of your procrastination or self-sabotage isn't laziness or a fixed mindset or some other character flaw...

The source of your procrastination and self-sabotage is a *forgiveness* opportunity. Your excruciating uncertainty is a lantern lighting your way to a breakthrough moment of understanding and clarity.

Perhaps you need to forgive your worst boss for providing feedback harshly.

Or the teacher who said you'd never amount to anything.

Or the parent who wasn't present.

Or the high school date who made you feel small when said you wanted to be an author.

In the past, I have motivated myself out of the ambivalence trap by understanding *opportunity cost,* or the idea that saying "no" to one thing is automatically saying "yes" to something else. When we say "no" to pursuing a professional journey that is joyful and fulfilling, we are saying *yes* to the joyless, unsatisfying work we're currently doing. Saying "no" to change is saying "yes" to status quo.

Look back at your list and identify what you've said *yes* to, and if those 'yeses' feels good to you. Maybe your no's created a *yes* to boundaries, self-care, or following through on something important to you. If so, nice! Here's a look at my list again, with the inherent yeses included:

- **NO**: Virtual coffee/lunch catch up | **YES**: Edit this very book
- **NO**: Taking on a pro bono client | **YES**: Honor my work and the value I bring to my clients
- **NO**: Letting the kids watch TV | **YES**: Impromptu trip to the local library
- **NO**: Hiring a certain publicity firm | **YES**: Trusting that I'll either feel great about a different firm, or be totally fine bootstrapping a while longer
- **NO**: Exercising | **YES**: Being less healthy than I'd like to be
- **NO**: Watching a comedian who's energy pulls me down | **YES**: Protecting my energy and making time for input that helps me do that
- **NO**: Getting to sleep on time | **YES**: Feeling groggy and cranky in the morning

I definitely feel better about some of those yesses than others.

As you look over your list, I hope you'll *follow the fear* if the *yes* didn't honor who you really are or what you want for yourself. Improv teachers often say "follow the fear" to new improvisers; it's a reminder that all the fun is waiting outside of their comfort zones. The only way to get outside your comfort zone is to acknowledge the fear and do the exact thing causing your heart to pound in your throat.

Sometimes fear is there to keep us safe... but the idea of "safe" is often shaped by our limiting beliefs. Remember the cat and the stove? Forgiveness work will help you calibrate your brain to a new understanding of *safe*... one that is based on actual safety, not keeping you small, trapped, and unhappy.

Curiosity. When you first start looking for limiting beliefs, you may find that they're hard to notice because they're cemented in your brain as *reality*. But they are there! Don't give up on rooting out limiting beliefs just because they're hard to identify.

For the longest time, "You can't trust men" was not a limiting belief for me—I viewed it as *reality* having been assaulted at such a young age in a place where I should have been safest.. and by someone I should have been able to trust: a teenager in the youth group of which my dad was the pastor. "You can't trust men" didn't sound at all like a "limiting belief," it sounded like a sad truth. That belief is validated from all corners of society. I'm pretty sure you can buy "Men suck" or "Men are the worst" tee shirts. (In fact, a quick Google search confirms: there are shirts.)

I also didn't view "You can't trust Christians" as a limiting belief. It just seemed very, very accurate. Plus, I had years' worth of additional supporting evidence.

My inability to identify these limiting beliefs was stealing my joy. I was being robbed of connection, with my husband and my childhood faith tradition.

Don't give up on curiosity. Limiting beliefs are there, and freedom is on the other side of recognizing them. There is *always* a limiting belief or two--or ten—embedded in a past painful experience. Otherwise, the situation wouldn't be hurtful to you still.

Until I started this work, I felt like I was being sliced in half by my memories of being abused at church. Now, the memories aren't *painful*. Before, when the memory was activated, my brain would go into overdrive: I would *flood* with sadness, anger, humiliation and fear.

But if we build on the idea of those painful feelings as *forgiveness guides*, which call our attention to something that hasn't been processed yet; if we recognize that the painful situation is ripe with limiting beliefs which cause us to feel isolated and hopeless... then we understand our reactions. My previous "flooding" makes perfect sense. There was *so much* I hadn't processed, and therefore so much asking for my attention so I could grow and heal.

It also makes sense that processing would deactivate that reaction. And it did.

What happened to me is still disgusting and wrong and horrible... but the situation no longer causes me physical pain. *Something can still be wrong without having its hooks dug into you.* Processing my limiting belief that I can't trust men has made it so I'm no longer worried about my ability to fully connect with and trust my husband. I no longer feel resentful about being raised in the church where my assault happened. I no longer have flashbacks or feel worried and uncomfortable when I'm changing a baby's diaper, or performing the other intimate tasks of parenting.

Doing this kind of forgiveness work allows you to enter the memory without flooding, because your focus is not on the details of what happened. Your focus is on the specific goal of hunting for limiting beliefs. Acknowledging those limiting beliefs de-fangs the memory. That way, if and when the memory resurfaces, you can choose to move on without flooding; you've already processed it. Your brain doesn't need to reopen the file and comb through the painful details.

Where focus goes, energy flows. If you focus on the details, you will reactivate pain. But this forgiveness work makes your reaction your choice: you can choose to open the file and rehash the grossness... but because of your healing work, you won't need (or want) to do that. You won't need to; you've already done your learning and growing and releasing.

This is why we only ever do curiosity work when we're in alignment. I also highly recommend creating an environment that's psychologically and physiologically safe for doing this kind of thinking. I like to plan it ahead of time, draw a hot bath, add some epsom salts, and get some 432 Hz music[15] playing.

That is what *chosen reflection* looks like versus *triggered reflection*. Triggered reflection is when something reminded you of a past event; involuntarily, you start unpacking a painful memory. Sometimes the trigger is something random, like an overdraft fee or a speeding ticket. Other times we find ourselves in situations directly analogous to past painful memories--having to fire someone reminds you of the time you were fired, or fighting with your spouse reminds you of your parents' fighting. Other times, people who are close to us push us (usually with the best of intentions) to reflect at times when we're not ready.

In any case: curiosity will lead you into a booby-trapped dessert of shame landmines if you enter into it out of alignment.

Reaction. One of my favorite examples of getting stuck in Reaction is in the movie *Frozen*. If you haven't seen it (hard for

---

[15] Some people say 432 hertz is a healing frequency. I don't know if that's true or not, but if you look for "432 HZ" on Spotify, you'll find some completely lovely and relaxing spa music. Worst case scenario, you'll sleep like a damn baby.

me to imagine as a mom to two young children... I've probably seen it 50 times), here's the basic gist:

Two sisters lose their parents, and since they are princesses, one will take over as Queen of Arendale (their Norwegian-inspired fictional kingdom) on her 18th birthday. That sister, Elsa, has special magic that she was forced to keep a secret. After having her secret exposed and being met with rejection and fear by the community, Elsa runs away and builds a giant ice castle where she can live in complete solitude in the mountains.

Now, even if you haven't seen the movie, I'm willing to bet you've heard the song *Let it Go* by Idina Menzel. If not, please do a quick YouTube search for the original song, and then search "Maddie and Zoe sing Let it Go." It will help you fully conceptualize the cultural phenomenon that is *Let it Go*... and it's just plain heartwarming. Go ahead--give yourself a brain break. You'll thank me later.

Okay, welcome back! Some of the lyrics in this song demonstrate perfectly the Reaction stage in the forgiveness process:

Let it go, let it go
Can't hold it back anymore
Let it go, let it go
Turn away and slam the door
I don't care what they're going to say
Let the storm rage on
The cold never bothered me anyway

As Elsa is singing these words, she's finally exploring her magic and finding out for the first time what she's capable of creating. It turns out, she can do some pretty impressive things! Elsa creates a snowman who comes to life, a beautiful ice staircase over a cliff, and an ice palace complete with an intricate fountain and chandelier.

"How is any of this bad?" you may be wondering. *"It sucks that she had to hide all this beautiful magic before--Arendale doesn't deserve her! They can suck it."*

Look, I get it. Arendale *can* suck it.
Elsa's experience with the *reaction stage* generated feelings of empowerment and confidence. Feeling powerful is way better than feeling ashamed and afraid!

That's why every stage is valuable—the reaction stage is an important moment for Elsa. She realizes that the thing she's been hiding from is actually a super power: that would be an important moment for anyone!

BUT the ability to do something impressive with your pain is not the same thing as dealing with your pain.

When Reaction shows up as a wave of empowerment, as in this example, it's easy to get stuck here because it looks good on the outside and it feels better than where we've been.

The trouble is that this manifestation of Reaction is a 5-Hour Energy Drink instead of a full night's sleep (or even better: a routine of getting good sleep regularly).

Reaction will give you a short-term boost; but it is hard, soul-crushing work to maintain that feeling of empowerment without doing the deeper work of continuing to process your hurt.

It's not true that you don't need anyone, or that you're fine to be alone in the cold (as we learn later in the movie). *"Forget you" and "forget me" are two sides of the same coin.* As you're practicing the energy of loathing and animosity, and thereby emotionally isolating yourself from the people around you, it's only a matter of time before those feelings turn inward.

When we stop people-pleasing, we feel empowered: we need that. But we also need the information, and the emotional regulation we get from the Curiosity, Confrontation, and Love stages.

In *Frozen,* chaos continues to unfold in Arendale and between Elsa and her sister Anna until they reconcile with the past. (This theme continues in *Frozen II* ...which I've also seen about 50 times. Because of my kids. Definitely, definitely, just because of the kids.)

Elsa's magic was never meant to be fearfully, shamefully suppressed. Until she came back down the mountain and confronted the situation fully, nobody could be safe. Not her. Not the people around her.

Sometimes we get stuck in the Reaction stage, not because the feelings of empowerment and self-righteousness are so appealing...but because heartache, guilt, and overwhelm have shown up. Sometimes our awareness of how deep our hurt truly goes, and maybe even how it's caused us to hurt others, is too much to bear.

Sometimes *shame* is what shows up in Reaction. Sometimes *worthlessness* is what shows up.

If you're currently trapped in a Reaction experience and moving into Curiosity feels like a quantum leap, it's time to ask for help.

Who you reach for in these vulnerable moments matters a lot. You need safe people who can *feed your curiosity* instead of *feeding your anger* or feeding your shame spiral. You need people who have earned the right to hear your story; people who speak the truth to you in love. You need people who can hold out a lantern and help you find your inner wisdom--not just tell you that you're right, or say the things you want to hear.

The people who love you may feed your anger the most, because they care so much or are also too close to the situation. *Talking with a neutral party, like a therapist or a hotline,*[16] *may prove more beneficial than talking to loved ones.*

There are three things to consider as you dive into this work.

1) The stages are written in a sequential order to make the forgiveness process more understandable, but *healing isn't linear.* Expect to move back and forth between stages as you work through your feelings and beliefs. I spent *years* exploring my toxic work situation with curiosity, always punting me back into reaction, which sometimes sent me into ambivalence before awareness would call my attention to another facet that was worth exploring.

2) These stages form an upward spiral. The more you practice, the easier it will become to move up the spiral.

When I'm leading a workshop and participants feel a great deal of resistance while reading the stages, it's because they're imagining trying to forgive the worst thing that's ever

---

[16] Many cities or counties have a local crisis hotline where you can speak to a trained professional for free even if you're not on the brink of suicide. There's a lot of help out there before you're in a worst-case scenario, and it's okay to utilize these services! If you're not aware of a local resource, you can call the National Suicide Prevention Lifeline which provides free, confidential, 24/7 support for mental health and crisis intervention: 1-800-273-8255

happened to them, or the thing that is presently causing the most pain and frustration.

Don't start there.

You wouldn't go to the gym for the first time and successfully bench press the *heaviest* weight plates. If you tried, you wouldn't be able to lift them at all and you'd assume it's impossible. OR, you would lift them enough to get them off the rack, and then immediately be squished to death.

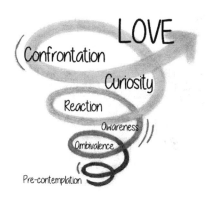

Don't get squished. Please. These things take time.

Start where you're safe. Start where the stakes are low enough that you can get a feel for each stage of the process. The goal is to gain an understanding of how to identify when you've moved from one stage to the next *without* dredging up emotional weight from the past that you're not yet prepared to safely lift!

3) It's easy to assume that there's a "right" amount of time to spend in each stage. There is not. Each stage has a job to do, and if we rush to the next stage out of a feeling of obligation, we will miss something.

Each stage holds new understandings for you. None of the stages are "bad." For instance, it's not bad to "only" be in Pre-Contemplation when considering a particular situation. As long as you're fully present in your life, and your intention is set on doing the work, you're in the right place wherever you are. Don't rush the process.

Don't rush the process.

Don't rush the process.

Did you catch that? I said it three times so it would really stand out to you. There's no hurry. *Be a good steward of the gifts of understanding that come to you at each stage.*

THE YES, AND FORGIVENESS NARRATIVE

Because I find journaling to be such a healing and helpful reflection tool, I created *The Yes, And Forgiveness Narrative*--a guided journaling exercise I have used many times. This exercise helps me attach to the narrative of love after I've fully processed, explored, and navigated the stages of forgiveness. It's only meant for personal use: I've never used this as a basis for a letter, email, or other form of written communication to anyone else. The exercise is just for me, to help me move forward with gentle curiosity.

Try writing a Yes, And Forgiveness Narrative for a situation you have fully processed. A Yes, And Forgiveness Narrative:

- Is specific and clear about what happened
- Assigns responsibility for actions appropriately
- Is honest about our true feelings, desires and hopes
- Indicates gratitude and intention
- Ends with a Yes, And. For example: Yes [_____ statement acknowledging the situation happened], AND [_____statement of agency or affirmation about

our future selves, and the bigger truth that we can be, do, and have anything we desire.]

Take the time to write this out rather than just thinking and reflecting. You can't write as fast as you can think, so writing forces you to slow down and give even more consideration to each piece of the narrative. Slowing down to write my thoughts has yielded me so many additional moments of clarity.

Pay careful attention to where you feel resistance. I often have trouble being specific and clear about what happened. I worry about what will happen if someone reads it and thinks "She's *this* upset about something as dumb as *that?!*"

No one is reading over your shoulder. Burn the page later if you need to. But don't duck out of any part of the exercise.

Here's an example of the Yes, And Forgiveness Narrative in action, helping me process the snowboard incident:

When I was a kid, I mustered the courage to say out loud that I wanted a snowboard for Christmas. In my heart, I knew it was unlikely, but I was brave and said it out loud anyway. Chewbacca[17] said "Your family probably can't afford it." and it made me feel small, embarrassed and defensive. I carried money shame for years after that experience.

It was supremely rude for him to say that. Also, I said horrifically rude things in middle school as well. The amount of resentment and hot lava rage I carried in my heart after that happened may have been disproportionate to the crime. I am responsible for

---

[17] I realize at this point I haven't given him a nom de guerre. This one seems appropriate. Just like Chewbacca, I used to be afraid of this cousin as a child; now as an adult, I have a whole new appreciation for him.

the grudges I nurse, and I am the one responsible for tapping into my own feelings of worthiness and optimism. It's no one else's job to carry that torch for me.

The truth is I hope to someday be where he is financially. I feel a bit of resentment and even fear sometimes. Fear that kind, open-minded people can't become as successful as aggressive, meanish people; what if his disregard for other's feelings and perspectives is part of WHY he is successful? What if I lack a killer instinct? What if I float like a butterfly AND sting like a butterfly?

I am so grateful for my work and the adventure that has been my career path, and it is my sincere intention to replace the jealousy I feel with happiness for his vast success as an entrepreneur. If he can do it, there's no reason I can't either. Success is in our DNA!

Yes, he hurt me deeply by judging my family and making me feel like the things I want aren't possible for me... AND I have grown past that limited understanding of the world. I am capable, courageous, willing, and worthy. All the good things are in store.

Now go write your own forgiveness narrative, ya filthy animal. (When was the last time you were called a 'filthy animal'? This is said to me at least weekly by my 6-year-old son, who watches the *Home Alone* movies year 'round. If I'm not a *filthy animal*, I'm a *law -breakin' knuckle head*. So. I definitely think I'm parenting well.)

FORGIVING THE SMALL STUFF TOO

When recognizably traumatic events happen, the need to forgive is more glaring and obvious. I shared that I'm a survivor of childhood sexual trauma, for which I've received years of therapy to help me process and heal. I have *easily* been able to identify that chapter of my life as my Everest of Forgiveness.

Little things can be trickier. When little things happen, we may not immediately recognize the need for forgiveness work, because we brush them off easily. But those little things are fueling the narrative we maintain about the people and places around us. Someone cuts us off in traffic, and we take note of their race, age, or vehicle type. When traveling, we stereotype entire cities (or even countries!) based on minor infractions we experience, which aren't representative of our trip as a whole. I recently heard someone expressing disdain for the entire country of Thailand because of the rudeness of one bus driver.

Forgiving the small things matters; doing this helps us maintain a narrative that matches our intentions and values. When we forgive the "little stuff," we practice the process of proactive forgiveness so we're better prepared to forgive the big things.

To give an example from my own life: people will say pretty much *anything* to people they don't know on the internet. When I was new to online video creation, I was caught off guard by a comment left on one of my posts.

"Who even comes up with this stuff??" the commenter asked... *with aggressive punctuation, which I've kept to emphasize his disgust!*

He went on to clarify that my use of the term *headspace* "triggered his psychobabble radar."

This man is a stranger to me. He's not knowledgeable about my field, and a quick visit to his profile allowed me to see the rage dumps he's left on *lots* of people's videos, articles, and blog posts.

For all of these reasons, it was fairly easy to recall the advice of the ineffably amazing Brené Brown for situations like this:

"If you are not also in the arena getting your ass kicked and being brave with your life, I am not interested in or open to your feedback."

This wasn't the first time someone had something negative to say in response to content I posted online, and it will certainly not be the last. Negative feedback is just part of putting yourself out there and allowing yourself and your work to be seen.

I gave myself that pep talk, blocked him, and moved on with my day.

But that night, after the kids were in bed, I pushed myself to stay up finishing client work instead decompressing after a long day of work and foster care drama. *I'm a hard worker,* I thought.

When my projects were done, I figured a *hard worker* wouldn't go to bed without scouring the kitchen sink. So, I did that too.

I stood there scrubbing, thinking self-righteous thoughts about my work ethic, my contributions to my social community, and how much positive feedback I've heard from my clients or other blog readers.

I'm good at what I do, I thought. *Plus, I'm a good friend. ...and I pay taxes and vote and recycle...* But unsurprisingly, my self-righteousness quickly devolved into a calculated observation of how I could be doing better.

We should give more to our church. I should volunteer more. It's been months since I called my Grandmother. I should know more about search engine optimization. I need to do better about batch recording videos. I should be posting content multiple times a day. What is a Facebook pixel? Every serious entrepreneur uses Google Analytics...why haven't I done that yet?"

I started revising the next day's docket--not based on what I needed in terms of self-care, or what I felt led to do... but based on what I *thought* I needed to get my mojo back.

That's when it hit me... *I'm in proving energy.*

Deep breath. *That man is more than who he was in that comment, and I am more than he thinks I am.*

That simple act of re-centering--and some quick EFT tapping--helped me get back on track and back into the zone for creating work that matters to me.

Even though this experience on social media was trivial, it still knocked at my worthiness.

I worked through the Forgiveness steps. I noticed that I was feeding biases as a result of this comment about my current and potential scene partners who fit his demographic, or who had similar professional backgrounds.

There are many subtleties in the human ego, and it's not always obvious when we slip into self-righteous, insecure posturing. Sometimes it's easier to lash out in response to a trigger, or to ignore your feelings without addressing their root cause.

We use dismissive adages like "That person is below you," or "They're not worth your time."

It's good to create boundaries around your heart, and to emotionally distance from the people hurling cheap insults at those of us who are in in the arena... *but when we completely dismiss triggering situations and our emotional responses without exploring, we miss out on forgiveness opportunities that could pay dividends in terms of our freedom, growth and joy.*

Forgiveness keeps us from sacrificing our alignment and the creative control of our lives. We have to identify our limiting beliefs to keep from creating vision-clouding biases and getting in our own way.

CHAPTER SUMMARY

Forgiveness is not about absolution; it is a process for healing and ridding ourselves of limiting beliefs and biases that keep us from establishing meaningful, authentic connections.

Forgiveness is absolutely, 100%, never ever a moral obligation. It is not the means by which we become "better people." Plenty of people do "good" things while living in misery because of their unforgiveness. Life is not supposed to be miserable!

We have to let go of the notion that certain things are "unforgivable." Feeling *justified* in our resentments will not bring us the freedom that forgiveness offers.

You can look for opportunities to prove that you're right or you can look for connection, but you can't do both. One of those options leads to self-righteous isolation, and one leads to effective peacemaking and conflict engagement. Forgiveness frees us up to choose the latter.

"Trivial things" still knock at our feelings of worthiness. Do the work of forgiveness even when it feels easier to characterize someone as a "meanie," or to decide that they're "below you."

CHAPTER 5: AND-ING WITH IMPACT

"In the long history of humankind (and animal kind too)
those who learned to collaborate and improvise
most effectively have prevailed."

~ *Charles Darwin*

In a way, forgiveness is the *yes* in the *yes, and* dance. It's the quiet, gentle, inward humility work that allows us to acknowledge and accept what currently exists so that we can *and* with impact.

Even if the forgiveness opportunities you've been thinking about are not directly work-related, like many of the examples in the previous chapter, YOU are the bridge. A heart full of self-doubt and resentment sits in your chest at your dinner table and in your board room, so your forgiveness work in either area benefits you as a *whole person*.

However, when the vastness of forgiveness work is focused onto leadership and onto culture shaping endeavors specifically, there are three particularly impactful shifts it can begin to motivate. The following three shifts are impactful to your company, but are also impactful to the world. These shifts put you on the leading edge of how we think about and *do* culture as a society!

A shift in your dominant focus from whatever it is now (revenue growth/ customer experience/ being viewed as powerful/ establishing a strong leadership reputation etc.) to *employee*

135

experience. AKA: your dominant intention will be to **support and honor your team members**, and as a result, you'll see that revenue growth and customer experience and whatever else matters for your version of success are not only still achieved, but they're achieved *better than they would have been* without this shift in focus.

A shift in your expectations for, and behavior during, **confrontation**. This dovetails into the first piece, because confrontation is *how* you support and honor your scene partners. I'll explain this more momentarily.

You will readily provide **accountability** for yourself and for others throughout the company. A culture cannot truly be healthy without accountability. Even for the highest performer. Even for the person who's been there the longest. Even if saying what needs to be said comes with a cost. Every good "culture intention" dies without accountability.

Support. Confrontation. Accountability.

We talked earlier in this book about the shift in focus from "the customer is always right" to "my employees are the most important thing." I told you to check out Vineet Nayar's book *Employees First, Customers Second,* and hopefully the book has already arrived at your house. I also highly recommend reading and learning about servant leadership. Two titles that have been particularly instrumental in my work are *The Servant* by James C. Hunter and *The Serving Leader* by Ken Jennings and John Stahl-Wert (fellow Pittsburghers by whom I'm honored to have been mentored.)

But what about the times when you're very, very sure someone at your company isn't trustworthy? What about the times when you didn't choose them and don't feel like you can get rid of them? What about the times when you have evidence demonstrating this person's imperfections and damaging behavior?

This predicament is the central focus of my work with companies, and where support, confrontation, and accountability come to center stage. Let's take a look at each individually:

SUPPORT

How do we honor the scene partners who do not behave honorably?

In the presence of dishonorable behavior, it is understandable to jump to confrontation or accountability. But there is a "level zero" belief I found to be transformational in how I go about those steps. It helps me bring true support into every conversation, even if clear boundaries must be set. Here is the belief: All humans (and please hear me say ALL humans) have love at their center.

I believe there are no exceptions to this at all. We call the act of making more people, *making love.*

...But wait... Even the folks who continue to spread misinformation about the vaccines that will save lives and help end a global pandemic? Yep.

Even the people protesting in front of my kids' school because of mask requirements put in place to prevent the need to return to virtual learning? Them too.

Even the people who made Peppa Pig?!

...Let's not get carried away. That is, without a doubt, the most painful children's show to sit through. Why are they having seizures on the floor at the end of every episode? Ridiculous! Give me Daniel Tiger or give me death.

I have spent the better part of two years in Peppa Pig purgatory while members of my community, who are otherwise sensible adults, refuse to wear a mask or do the bare minimum to end this madness.

Is this extremely frustrating to me? Of course.

Are these things indicative of people with no intelligence, empathy, or concern for global well-being? NO!

I find that behavior confusing and harmful, but as someone who once emailed the staff of Bluffton University with urgent information about the end of times...I recognize their humanity, their fear, and most importantly: the love at the core of who they are. I'm also deeply aware of their parallel confusion about my choice to be vaccinated; we just don't live inside the same factual reality.[18]

I know some people find this hard to accept. When we look around, our news feeds are full of examples indicating that people do NOT have love at their center. But even the hateful, dismissive memes (coming from liberal and conservative corners and everywhere in between) and social posts make sense to me, based on what I've already shared in this book

---

[18] The Social Dilemma provides a lot of context about how this came to be; it's definitely worth a watch if you're also feeling perplexed about how loving and intelligent people can be 100% convinced of opposite "facts." My level of empathy as well as awareness about some needed adjustments to my social media consumption increased considerably after watching.

about limiting beliefs. We all experience hurt and trauma that result in the formation and acceptance of limiting beliefs; those beliefs often harden into "soul plaque" without our knowledge.

The places we're born and the cultures to which we're exposed contributes to that soul plaque. We inherit cathedrals, trauma, and beliefs from our parents about the systems and people around us. As we grow, our limited first-hand experiences tempt us to call the stories we receive "objective truth."

It has helped me, in these intense emotional times, to remember that people might purchase a bumper sticker or post something on Facebook with the intention of ruffling feathers or being hurtful--but they don't *hold beliefs* with the intention of being hurtful. They hold beliefs because of their lived experiences. When I see posts that are particularly troubling (from my friends on both sides of the political aisle and everywhere in between), I try to ask myself "What belief prompted them to post this?" It helps me fight the urge to get caught up in their emotional momentum and be an "equal and opposite reaction[19]."

I invite you to consider the possibility that that core of love is *who we really are*. And everything else is learned behavior that morphs over time, and can morph into closer alignment with our deepest truth: love.

This is a critical distinction, because if we believe the people around us--disagreeable as we may find them--*are love* at their core, then our entire perspective on our relationships shifts.

---

[19] I offered a free training a while back pairing Newton's laws of motion with mindful improv and how this combo can guide us through the emotional momentum we experience in confrontation. I'm not bragging, but it's the best training that exists on the internet. You can find a replay of that training at andbeyondimprov.com/bookresources

As leaders, we can begin to see that our job is not to ask our team members to CHANGE who they are--a daunting task for even the most self-aware. However, we can invite our team members to grow into *more of who they are*. This is a doable ask. And one that is achieved through confrontation and accountability.

If we want to see more love in the world, we have to encourage more people to tap into the love they already have. It's an exhausting thing, to believe it's your job to fill the world with love by pouring constantly from your own cup. That's a good way to get burnt out, or to find yourself leaning into a hero complex that serves no one.

When we truly understand that all people are love at their center, and that all people are capable of tapping into that source, we begin to understand two helpful things when it comes to engaging confrontation and disagreement:

1. We are more alike than we are unalike (to quote the sage poet, Maya Angelou in her poem *Human Family*)
2. The world is *already* filled with love. It's not that we need more love, it's that we need to tap into the love we already have more often.

Of the many groups to which we assign Earth's inhabitants, I believe there are only two classifications that matter: people who--in this moment--are tapped into their center of love, and people who are not.[20]

---

[20] In March of 2019 I had the pleasure of attending an Esther (Abraham) Hicks workshop in Ft. Lauderdale, Florida -a place that has become very special to me. I nearly fell over hearing her share this same exact idea, although in slightly different, slightly more Abrahamic terms. When something is true, it pops up all over!

If we're being honest with ourselves, we each spend time in both of those categories. In fact, we jump from one to the other daily; sometimes even hourly!

If we aim to see real change, we need to spend less time being sure that we're *right* and more time being sure we're *tapped into our center of love.*

I know this for sure--you're not going to foster the growth of a single person by insisting that you're *right*. But you've got a much better chance of helping someone grow when you're tapped into your center of love.

When the theory that love is at the center of every person first entered my mind, it was hard for me to accept. I didn't grow up with this naïve-sounding, excessively spiritual belief. The picture of concentric circles making up the human identity with love at the center (which I have shared on the book resources page, andbeyondimprov.com/bookresources) came to me while I was creating the *Freedom Through Forgiveness* workshop content.

When I saw this picture, I immediately felt energized, encouraged, and hopeful about the future of humanity. But when I thought about saying this theory out loud to strangers who had paid money for me to teach them about forgiveness...I felt less energized and hopeful!

I could already imagine the eye rolls and dismissive glances; I could already imagine the rebuttals and the debates that would ensue.

But then I remember *ME*. I remember spreading conspiracy theories that were rooted in both religious fear mongering and racism. I remember (with a heavy heart and lump in my throat even now) things I used to say and believe about gay people. I remember the dismissive way I spoke about other people's cultures and faith traditions outside of Christianity. I remember my own fakery and inauthenticity while trying desperately to belong somewhere. I remember betraying the trust of friends for fleeting moments of connection with other people. There are people who knew me then, who would easily present evidence that says I am a hateful, racist bigot and a flaky friend. For these things, I remain deeply remorseful.

But there is a deeper truth. Those things were never *all* that I was! In fact, my very sincere desire to understanding what it means to be "good" prompted me to ask questions, read books, take classes and make friends with people who helped me come to a new, more loving understanding.

As I continued to research and interview folks whose work is helping people tap into their center of love instead of continuing to build lives of hatred, fear or violence, this theory that *love is at the center of all people* continued holding up. I read stories or even directly interviewed people who have had direct peace building roles in war torn countries, people who help young men leave gangs, people who guide others out of cults or radicalized beliefs, and people who are working to end systemic racism in our country and around the world.

You can see some of these interviews in the Peace Building Conspirators Facebook group – it's a diverse, multifaith, nonpartisan online community I started in 2020 where we talk about how to make the world a better place. It's free to join and I hope you do!

So with this idea in tow, let's explore the second component of *and-ing with impact*: confrontation.

CONFRONTATION

If you know my work, you know confrontation is my jam. Early on, I made an entire e-course with meaningful content and poorly edited video on the subject. It's called *The Art of Confrontation*. It's still available for purchase despite its imperfections.

For a long time, I called the method I teach for engaging confrontation *the backwards approach*. Then I was informed by a pervert (whom I adore) that it sounds like an academic term for doggy style sex ... and I was thoroughly embarrassed. I had already scandalized many people at that point.

Now I call this approach the Gold Standard for Relationship Building Through Confrontation, or GSFRBTC. (I bet you wish we could go back to *the backwards approach*, huh?! IT'S TOO LATE. I'VE ALREADY YES, ANDED.)

Remember when we talked about forgiveness and I said that it's a *prerequisite for effective confrontation?* That's what makes this method backwards.

Historically, we've internalized graphic imagery associated with confrontation, e.g. "I spoke up and got shot down." "Someone blew up at work today." "The situation erupted." "The shit hit the fan."

We've also been taught to think about confrontation as the determining factor in whether or not someone *earns* our forgiveness. "We'll have it out, and if that person apologizes well enough I'll forgive him."

This approach puts our freedom, growth, and joy in someone else's hands. It also assumes that if that person changes, we'll notice and appreciate the shift.

That's mostly <u>not</u> how we roll. We roll like Jonah-- a character from an ancient Hebrew story who was instructed (by God!) to help the Assyrians in Nineveh become more loving, ethical people. Jonah delivers the message, *and the people actually change.* But instead of rejoicing in a job well done and appreciating the human capacity for growth, Jonah sits on a hillside waiting to see God smite their city anyway.

Jonah had hated these people for so long, and had practiced self-righteous judgement and resentment for so long, that he couldn't pivot as quickly as the Assyrians did. The story ends with Jonah sitting on a hillside, alone in the hot sun, praying to die; death would be better than seeing his perceived enemies thriving in the grace of God.

I think I speak for all of us when I say: DAMN.

We like to see people get what they deserve. We like to argue the case for their smiting in the safety of our social circles. We like to feel justified in our continued resentment, even at the expense of our own thriving!

This is a dangerous tendency. We cannot cultivate the desire for failure, pain, and destruction for someone else without cultivating failure, pain, and destruction in our own experience. We get what we focus on... so shift your focus, Jonah!

Fortunately there is another, way better, way more joyful, way more productive method to engage conflict.

At this point, you already know confrontation is really a piñata (not a battle or explosion). When you see confrontation developing, you already know to break out the party hats instead of the battle armor and prepare to collect some critical, delightful, and even surprising gifts.

But I want to offer some technical know-how for applying mindful improv to these delicate moments. There are four culture-defining instances where confrontation is happening, even if you wouldn't call it that.

- When you are giving difficult feedback
- When you are receiving difficult feedback
- When someone is self-advocating in front of you
- When you are facilitating creative collaboration

I call these *the four critical moments,* because these are the moments when your team members decide whether they are valued and appreciated or tokenized.

These are the moments when people decide to keep showing up as their best selves, or decide to start passively collecting a paycheck. These moments determine whether people believe it's safe to be vulnerable and brave enough to ask for what they want--or if they're better suited responding to a recruiter on LinkedIn.

Culture isn't forged at your team-building escape room night. Culture is forged through confrontation, which occurs in these four moments. It happens in the times when folks are choosing to be vulnerable and sincere, despite their expectation that they will be met with opposition in some form.

That's my working definition of confrontation. I like it, because it creates space for the numerous exchanges where the confrontee isn't feeling the same emotional weight as the confronter. Our life experiences determine how we feel heading into a conversation, so it's pretty normal for one person to view something as a confrontation and another person to view something as "coffee talk."

Confrontation isn't necessarily about *disagreement*, it's about *expectations*.

What you've already learned about The Core Five Mindful Improv Skills for Life, alignment, and forgiveness work is enough to guide you through critical moments 2-4. But in my experience, it's helpful for leaders to pay special attention to critical moment #1: giving difficult feedback.

In my experience, there are three primary approaches to giving feedback. They are confrontation (this should be the first reach whenever possible), intervention, and attack.

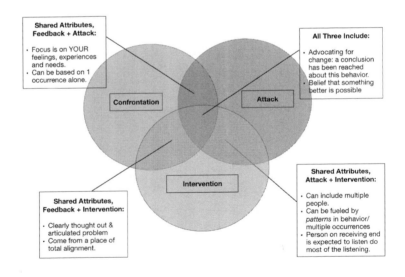

Shared Attributes, Feedback + Attack:
- Focus is on YOUR feelings, experiences and needs.
- Can be based on 1 occurrence alone.

All Three Include:
- Advocating for change: a conclusion has been reached about this behavior.
- Belief that something better is possible

Confrontation

Attack

Intervention

Shared Attributes, Feedback + Intervention:
- Clearly thought out & articulated problem
- Come from a place of total alignment.

Shared Attributes, Attack + Intervention:
- Can include multiple people.
- Can be fueled by *patterns* in behavior/ multiple occurrences
- Person on receiving end is expected to listen do most of the listening.

Each approach has potential to overlap the other approaches, and it's important to notice when that's happening. Feedback is received most effectively when it is delivered intentionally, and when the deliverer is squarely in their zone of intention.

I like to use this visual demonstration to help explain the way these three approaches can overlap:

Here are the key characteristics of each approach to help you better understand what's happening. Know which approach you're taking to providing feedback, and stay aligned with your intention when delivering the difficult feedback to a team member.

Confrontation:

- Rooted in *curiosity and desire for exploration* instead of being rooted in the desire to share your narrative about a situation. There's a time and a place for narrative-sharing...but that's not how confrontation is most effective, nor how dialogue is best facilitated.
- Is predicated upon a single action/comment or a *very recent* detection of a pattern
- The primary goal is about YOU, the confronter, and making your needs/boundaries/questions etc. known.
- Handled one on one
- Includes a balance of information input from both parties
- Ends with clarity on opportunities for additional building, or clarity on the need for release

Intervention:

- Comes from a place of true concern for the *confrontee*, or person being confronted

- Is predicated upon a substantial pattern of past behavior and past confrontations
- The primary goal is about the health/success of the confrontee
- Can include multiple stakeholders in the situation, and can even include a neutral mediator
- The confrontee is asked to simply listen
- The desired outcome has been understood and agreed upon by all stakeholders involved
- Ends with an offer of help, and a request that the confrontee accept that offer. Also offers very clear boundaries and consequences, which have also been previously agreed upon by all stakeholders

Attack:

- Comes from a place of fear, and leaves the confrontee sharing that sense of fear
- Often reactionary; it's easy to slip into attack once you've initiated one of the other approaches, and if you're reacting to something sensitive or hurtful in the moment.
- Often uses accusatory and/or hyperbolic language, e.g.: "I'm not the only one who thinks this," or "You *always* do this"
- Lacks a clearly defined SPARK goal (this is what I teach my clients when they're preparing for confrontation. A good SPARK goal is Specific, Personal, Aligned, Relevant, and Knowledge-Informed)
- Leans heavily on a cathedral narrative

My background is in social work; this has given me a special appreciation for the validity of the *intervention* approach, when someone is in need of urgent help in order to make safe choices. However, it's important to understand that there are methods and procedures that make intervention effective when it's appropriate. When we step into intervention without the evidence of past patterns that need transformation, we create what I call a *pseudo-intervention* that is not productive in the least.

In a *pseudo-intervention,* we make our scene partner feel condescended to. The confronter plays the role of the savior by overstating the degree of concern they feel for the other person. You've probably heard this common example many times:

Voldemort[21]: Hey is everything okay?

Dumbledore: Yes, I'm just running 5 minutes late

Voldemort: Okay, we were just worried since we hadn't heard from you.

BULL. HONKEY. You're not worried. You're annoyed that Jim sat on the toilet scrolling through social media for 20 minutes this morning instead of getting to work on time.

Curiosity can help us avoid this. Ask yourself: do I *really* feel concerned for this person? Or am I irritated about something, and pretending to be concerned feels like the most socially appropriate way to bring it up?

Here's a delightfully embarrassing example of pseudo intervention from my own life: when I was 21, I came home from college with my first ever hickey. My sweet mom noticed right

---

[21] Coming up with example names is the hardest part of writing a book. I've never actually read the Harry Potter series, so I'm not 100% sure if this conversation happened between these characters... but probably.

away and was too embarrassed to say anything. She cried herself to sleep, and the next morning my dad confronted me.

"Hey Annie, your mom and I talked last night, and we're a little worried about you."

I had made no effort whatsoever to hide the hickey, so I knew what was happening.

"Little ol' me? Whatever for, Father?" (Best recollection of my exact words.)

"We're wondering if there's maybe something going on with your liver?"

Decidedly *not* what I was expecting.

"…Um, I don't think there's anything wrong. Why would you ask that?"

"Well, we noticed that spot on your neck —"

"And you assumed it was a *liver spot?!*" I shouted.

Things escalated quickly, and I stormed out of the room. I was perfectly situated at that angsty, not-really-an-adult stage where 85% of my interactions with my parents ended with me shouting the words "I'm an adult!" …just before driving off in their car, full of gas that they bought, and complaining to my boyfriend about it on a cell phone that they paid for.

While I have to assume feigning concern about a liver condition in order to address your college-age daughter's hickey is *not* a common experience, *pseudo-intervention* certainly is.

It's easier to pretend to be *concerned* than to be honest that you're *upset*. If we're honest that we're upset, we have to account for *why* we're upset, and that's vulnerable!

The truth is that my parents were *sad* that I was growing up. They were *afraid* about the repercussions of me having physical relationships. They were *angry* that I wasn't following the "no second basing until you're married and 47 and barely want to anymore" rule. ...and truthfully, they were probably also hurt because I was being a serious anal crevice about all of these things.

Saying how we really feel is hard. And there's a good chance that in 30 or 40 years, when my kids are second basing for the first time, I'll forget everything I've written in this book and stage an intervention alongside a hepatologist.

Pseudo-intervention is a problem *outside* of parenting as well.

It's easier to bring along a friend, or an HR rep (or a hepatologist) and pretend the pseudo-intervention is about accountability or legal protections...when really it's about the difficulty of saying "This didn't work for me." or "This hurt my feelings."

It's easier, or safer, to assert power in the form of attack, or to use condescending and overblown language, rather than sit face-to-face with a scene partner who has over-stepped, under-performed, or otherwise transgressed...and to treat that scene partner with honor.

Good people pseudo-intervene or slip into attack when they're feeling surprised or vulnerable. Attacking is not their intention, but that does not diminish the damaging impact of the behavior.

Communication is *receiver oriented*, so it's important to remember that your intention is less important than your execution when giving difficult feedback. If you slip outside of *confrontation* and into *attack,* your scene partner will feel defensive. If you slip into *intervention*, your scene partner will feel condescended to and annoyed.

If our goal is to help our scene partner grow so they can start building something amazing with us, we need to offer the information *in a receivable manner.* This is where getting into alignment, using The Core Five, and doing forgiveness work to remove the soul plaque of cathedrals, bias, and projection will be your saving grace.

I used to have so many *guidelines* for confrontation. I used to make "quick scripts" and provide a lot of infrastructure for clients to use in moments of confrontation. I don't do that anymore, because I now realize the most important thing is for you to *get into alignment and trust what happens after that.*

You have everything you need inside of you to navigate the *courage and humility* dance during confrontation. Remember that you're dancing. Bring a brick, not a cathedral, and trust your aligned instincts as the rest unfolds.

ALL CONFRONTATIONS ARE NOT CREATED EQUAL

The GSFRBTC [22] can be applied to big or small hurts, frustrations, miscommunications, etc. However, confrontation doesn't make for better relationships when we go too small on something big or too big on something small. Sometimes a

---

[22] Gold Standard For Relationship Building Through Confrontation. Remember? The new name for ~~doggy style~~ the backwards approach to confrontation?

quick text saying "Hey, just noticed the stapler was in the wrong spot. Here's where it should go," is the best way to honor your scene partner. Sometimes it's okay to send an email to give more detailed instructions. Other times a phone call is best.

I created the chart below because I LOVE CHARTS. Like, I really love them. I made this one to help me gauge how I should respond in the wake of a frustrating/hurtful situation or opportunity for feedback.

This chart offers a visual way to parse how deeply I'm impacted by the situation and how much there is to accomplish, and therefore, what means of communication will best serve that particular situation.

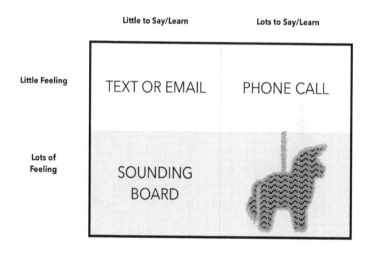

	Little to Say/Learn	Lots to Say/Learn
Little Feeling	TEXT OR EMAIL	PHONE CALL
Lots of Feeling	SOUNDING BOARD	

Hearkening back to the concept of the piñata: When there are lots of feeling and lots to say and learn, it's "party time;" move forward with face to face, 1:1 communication whenever possible.

This chart has helped me avoid causing the "Hey, can we talk?" anxiety for others when it's not necessary. When a more in-depth conversation is needed, this chart helps me prep the right environment for confrontation to be meaningful.

INITIATING PRODUCTIVE, HEALTHY CONFRONTATION SCENES

Once you've decided that *it's party time*, how can you initiate the confrontation? What should you say or not say? You'll have these answers when you're in alignment... but I do have some pointers.

First, I recommend that *whenever possible*, confrontation be handled face to face and one on one. Here's the process I use:

Step 1: Reach out via text, email, or other written communiqué to request face time.

At this initial stage, it's important to be clear that something is upsetting you, but not be specific about the details. The reason is that if you're overly specific at this stage, you'll invite an immediate rebuttal via email, which will invite a response from you, and before you know it, you're hashing it out via email or text. This is not ideal because you've lost some of the key ingredients for building human connection: eye contact, tone, nonverbal communication, and the shared energy that is present when two people decide to share space.

Step 2: Choose a location that honors both of you.

Although I am an eternal optimist and proudly hold a "things are getting better every day" worldview, the reality is that gender dynamics, workplace hierarchy, and social politics must be considered when choosing the location for a delicate conversation. While it's tempting to ignore those factors in favor of a world where none of that matters, we'll risk not having a truthful conversation if we don't pay attention to some of these logistics. Here are some location criteria to consider:

- Is this location a common hangout for other co-workers, church goers, or mutual acquaintances? If so, it's not a good spot. It's painfully awkward to run into someone you know mid-confrontation (lived experience!)
- Can either person leave when they need to? This is an important part of psychological safety. For this reason, it's not ideal to do it at either person's home or in either person's office.
- Is this location private? This may seem obvious, but in the world of open office floor plans, privacy can be harder to accommodate than it seems. How you communicate when you know other people are listening or can see you is not the same as how you communicate when you have privacy. The perception of having an audience shifts you into *performance* headspace, and in moments of confrontation, it's crucial for you to be in the vulnerable, authentic, collaborative headspace.
- Does this location feel safe to both parties? This is about emotional safety and physical safety. I once initiated this sequence of confrontation, and my scene partner suggested we have the conversation in the parking lot behind our building because there was not a meeting room available. Due to the power hierarchy between us, I felt obligated to agree to this, but it was very uncomfortable to be alone with this man in the parking lot. So, the moral of that story is… don't pick a parking lot.

If you have concerns about where to meet, I recommend suggesting at least two locations in your ask for face time. Allow the other person to suggest an alternative if desired.

WHAT TO DO WHEN YOU GET TO THE TABLE:

Step 3: Start with instructional curiosity

The concept of *Instructional curiosity* is important, because this is how we avoid the common pitfall of asking a *loaded question* instead of a *curious question*. Instead of asking "Do you know why we're here?", start by coming clean about the specifics of what is on your mind.

When I met with my friend from the piñata story in Chapter 1, I started out by offering a simple, clear brick:

"When we were at the bar last week, and we somehow got on the subject of the Bible, I felt really attacked by what you said. Do you know what I'm talking about?"

Be clear about what happened from your point of view, how you felt about it, and then *stop* and check in. Maybe this person doesn't remember what you're talking about at all! (Hint: this is why it matters to be timely about when to initiate confrontation. I've had friends for whom I care deeply wait *six months* to confront me about something I said that was hurtful. When we got to the confrontation, I truly had no recollection of the event at all.)

Step 4: Listen with a willingness to pivot

As your scene partner is responding, it's important that you're truly listening; truly willing to go with them where they're going. If you're secretly planning your rebuttal the whole time they're speaking, you're not really listening. If you're just waiting for your turn to talk and make it about you again, you're not really listening.

Again, we must ask: "What do I really want?" If you want the situation to improve, you must understand that *your scene partner's response to your offering of information holds all of the information you need to build what's next.* Their response is pointing at what needs to be worked on. If they deflect, you can ask why. If they change the subject, you can ask why. If they are silent, you can survive that. Silence is not an emergency. Silence is still full of information. Be patient. Receive what your scene partner is giving you.

Don't come to the table with an agenda; come with a goal for growth. This is how you "win" every time. When you're more attached to seeing things improve than you are to receiving an apology or gaining this person's approval, you can truly come alongside and build a deeper connection or at least increase your understanding.

Step 5: Edit as needed

In improv, an *edit* is when one or multiple players end one scene and move to the next. Often, this looks like one improviser running across the front of the stage, which signals the improvisers engaged in a scene to clear the stage and make room for whatever is next...which they will discover together.

Knowing when to edit is an important skill for improvisers. When you first get started, it's tempting to wait far too long to edit a scene. It feels rude! It feels like interrupting! Also, if a scene has been going on for a while and isn't going well, you may think: "I can't edit now! I want to give them a chance to find their scene." (And that's as it should be at the beginning of an awkward scene... but six or seven minutes in: put them out of their misery.) Lastly, it feels really good to edit after a huge laugh ... but waiting for that laugh isn't always a good idea. If you wait for the big reaction, you risk letting the scene run past its momentum.

Editing at the right time is truly an art form. So how do you know when to edit? Here's the guideline: edit *as soon as you think you should!*

Seriously.

That's what they teach you. Your first impulse to edit the scene is the right impulse. Everything after that is the unhelpful waffling and second guessing that leads to weak improv.

I want you to grasp the importance of *knowing when to edit* in life, too. Remember that confrontation doesn't have to be resolved all at once! It's okay to notice when you and your scene partner have done all the productive work you can do in the moment; then, clear the stage for new inspiration.

When a scene is edited in improv, we can always return to those characters/themes/ideas later in the show. We say "nothing is forgotten in improv!" Few things are as delightful as a perfectly timed *call back* (when the players on stage bring back a joke or idea from earlier in the show).

Remember that not everyone who is on the stage (literally or metaphorically) wants to be there. Pride and pent-up rage or resentment get in the way of our ability to "yield our time" as readily as we should. An edit can come as a relief to your scene partner.

Imagine this scenario: you're in a board room. For the entirety of the meeting, one person is shaking his head, muttering under his breath, and alternating between sitting on the very edge of his chair (ready to attack) or sitting back with arms folded crossed his chest.

After this goes on for a bit, something finally sets him off. He explodes: "I can't sit here and take this anymore! This is total BS!"

After railing for 30 seconds, he is met with expressions of discomfort and uncertainty from the others in the room.

"I'm not the only one who feels this way!" he protests. "Everyone in my department agrees with me!"

You may be tempted to sit back and allow the outburst to continue. It seems as though the disgruntled scene partner *wants* the floor; that he *wants* to share this perspective. But if you're a leader or committed culture protagonist in this situation there are several questions to ask:

Is this person able to represent their perspective at the caliber it deserves in this moment?

Am I allowing additional consequences into the equation by allowing this to scene to continue?

Does this person *still* want to be the center of attention, or has this gotten out of hand in a way that was not likely his/her intention?

When corporate teams bring me in to teach my confrontation processes, I often play a game I call *Hot Spot Collaborative Story*. This game combines a few classic improv games that work together to build on some of the most critical skills of confrontation.

Hot Spot Collaborative Story: The group stands in a circle and one person is in the middle. This person initiates a made up, never-before-heard story. The group takes turns tagging out the person in the middle and taking their place, as they feel inspired by the story. They simply run into the middle of the circle and tag the person's shoulder to do this. However, they must pick up the story *exactly* where their predecessor left off, using the same words *verbatim*.

There are several goals to this game:

- Collectively tell a cohesive story with a clear beginning, middle, and end.
- Notice when you're planning something out of fear, rather than listening to what's being said and being organically inspired.
- Trust your creative instincts and your brain's ability to continue giving you new ideas
- Free yourself up to receive those ideas by practicing alignment

But most importantly for our purposes right now, this game is about *sacrificial support*.

It's about understanding that sometimes the person who has the floor is *suffering*, and the merciful thing to do is tag them out and give them a break! It's about feeling the joy of receiving support from your teammates rather than being left hanging and feeling foolish… but it's also about owning your space and knowing that your contributions are *not* foolish.

I love watching leaders play this game. I love watching them dread their inevitable turn in the middle. I love watching them *hate it* the first time the story makes no sense, when they're pretty sure improv is the worst thing ever. I love hearing them discuss what was difficult, what feelings they experienced, and what kept them cemented on the sidelines. And I especially love seeing them engage the game on a whole new level the second time around.

ACCOUNTABILITY

At the time of this writing, *accountability* is a word firmly in the zeitgeist. There is a profound understanding that leaders are accountable for culture, and that it's not acceptable to duck responsibility for building a diverse, inclusive, healthy culture. It isn't okay to keep people around who are poisoning the water hole, treating others badly, and refusing to grow with the times. The days of *she gets funded, so she stays* are quickly moving behind us as a society.

Accountability cannot prevail in a context where it is paid lip service, but where there are no structures to ensure it happens.

I implore you to get into alignment, listen with curiosity, and honor the scene partners at your company or on your team by implementing brave policies to which you will hold everyone accountable. Good intentions don't create a culture of accountability; follow-through does.

I'm not an HR consultant, and this is not a book of policy recommendations, so I don't have a bullet list of to-do items for you. My advice is that you'll know what you need to do when you're in alignment. And if your aligned intuition says: *I need to learn more about this*, I highly recommend following Claude Silver, Chief Heart Officer at Vayner Media, for inspiration. At Vayner Media, they are prioritizing their people and building a culture where *love* is not an unfamiliar word; and they're doing this to become successful beyond imagination.

It's pretty inspiring stuff!

I do have advice regarding the logistics of *how* to hold people accountable. In the section above, you learned some of my processes for giving difficult feedback. This is a key part of accountability.

But in some situations, you may be able to support a team member's behavior modification journey via a coaching role. In this case, you can blend what you've already learned about mindful improv with some key tenets of *motivational interviewing* to facilitate successful growth.

CRASH COURSE IN MOTIVATIONAL INTERVIEWING (MI)

While I consider myself one of MI's most dedicated fan-girls, I do not consider myself an expert. I am not a MINT (Motivational Interviewing Network of Trainers) certified trainer, and the way I implement MI in my work now is certainly a blended approach; I call it *motivational interviewing and mindful improv*, or MIAMI. Retreats forthcoming, remember?!

The spirit of MI is to come alongside the person with whom you are talking, and help them notice and build upon their own internal motivation to change. Note that it's called motivational *interviewing*, not motivational *lecturing*. The point is to *ask good questions*, to listen well, and to simply mirror back to someone the most helpful pieces of what they're already doing.

It's not your job to lecture, guilt, or externally motivate this person to do what you think they should do.

Earlier in the book, I mentioned that it's human nature to play devil's advocate and poke holes in someone else's suggested solutions. But the better approach is to *ask brave questions* and be as solution-focused as possible. Highlight every piece of evidence the person mentions that could indicate that a desired change is possible, and even probable.

EG: if the person mentions that they've quit smoking, reflect back how much courage and discipline that took. Courage and discipline are the same skills they need to make whatever change the person now desires. Remind the person how they've already deployed courage and discipline!

Remember to use your OARS when engaging in Motivational Interviewing:

O - Open-ended questions
A - Affirmations
R - Reflections
S - Summaries

Open Ended Questions: Ask questions like "What does ___ mean to you?" or "What's at stake for you if ____ stays the same?" instead of "Did you know that ___ is a violation of the employee handbook?" or "Are you committed to this relationship?" Ask questions that invite the other person to elaborate on his/her perspective, rather than giving yes/no answers.

Affirmations: Give positive feedback. This is important for building a rapport, and for making sure the other person knows that he/she is seen as a whole person beyond the specific attitude, belief or behavior in question.

As someone who has completed extensive training in Parent Child Interactive Therapy (PCIT) with my daughter, I can vouch for the effectiveness of affirming behaviors I want to see continue (in PCIT lingo, this is called *labeled praise*). For example:

Unlabeled Praise: "Good job!"

Labeled Praise: "Thank you for asking me for what you needed so nicely. I really like it when you say *please*."

Another example:

Unlabeled Praise: "Good job!"

Labeled Praise: "I really liked the pace and flow of your presentation this morning-- you had the perfect balance of content and engagement."

Reflections: Repeat back something that's just been said in the person's own words. This lets them know you're listening; sometimes providing an echo of what's just been said is all it takes for someone to *hear it differently*. This simple action can pave the way for big change.

Summaries: Interject every so often to summarize what's been said; this serves the other person and you. You want to be sure you've understood them, and that you're not interpreting anything that's been said differently than it was intended. Summarizing lets the other person know you were listening and gives them an opportunity to clarify or add anything that's been forgotten.

Once you summarize what they've just said, check in: "Did I get that right?" and/or, "Is there anything I'm forgetting or misunderstanding?"

Through reflecting and summarizing, you can practice the five key strengths of MI:

- Empathy
- Optimism (especially about this person's inherent self-efficacy)
- Acceptance of resistance
- Preventing argument
- Establishment of discrepancy

EMPATHY: This part is critical. If you're reading this book, you're no doubt a kind person with the best intentions for creating a beautiful world for everyone. You may have the self-concept that you're an *empathetic* person.

But empathy isn't about your good will toward others. Empathy is about your ability to relate to their *experience and perspective*.

When you're providing feedback or coaching a team member via motivational interviewing, *empathy is critical*. Before you push your agenda, or provide statistics backing up your perspective, make time to establish empathy; "It's hard to go through a change in leadership. Thank you for hanging in during this transition period." Or "Things have been so busy lately, and I know it's frustrating when communication gets lost in the chaos. I feel that tension too." Whatever is actually sincere and specific is good. You are a great improviser.

You increase the likelihood of attaining your desired results when you prioritize *strengthening the relationship* over *proving your correctness*. Empathy is how you strengthen the relationship: true empathy, sans agenda.

OPTIMISM ABOUT SELF EFFICACY: We often think that it's the responsibility of the leader, the teacher, the pastor, or the parent to motivate others to achieve. When we approach motivation that way, we make the job harder.

Each of us is motivated toward *something*. When leaders find out what that something is for the person on the other side of the table, and tap into the person's inherent desire to achieve that thing, they won't need to *create the motivation* for them. The motivation will present itself naturally.

What does the person *want*? More money? Responsibility? A certain job title? More travel? A different degree? For you to address a toxic person in the office?

If the person believes they can't have these things, then their desire *for* them becomes an obstacle to motivation. By removing these obstacles, you'll give the person opportunities to perform at a new level.

This is one of the core concepts of servant leadership: remove the obstacles and meet the needs. If you push, push, push to motivate, you may be pushing your team members *away*.

We've just scratched the surface of motivational interviewing. I believe it is *the* most effective way to support and facilitate behavior modification. Because I believe in MI so much, I have a free, hour-long webinar on my website called Encouraging Change that offers specific advice for utilizing this method. You can find it at andbeyondimprov.com/encouragingchange. Check it out!

IMPROV PRACTICE ACTIVITY: THE DOLPHIN TRAINER GAME

Occasionally, I play a game called Dolphin Trainer with my clients to help them practice this skill. You can try it with your group! In this game, one person leaves the room (she or he is the dolphin) and the rest of the group (the trainers) decide one task that the dolphin must complete when they return. For example: they must do a jumping jack, or mark an X on the dry erase board, or play an air guitar.

Once the group has decided, the dolphin is called back in. As soon as she or he enters the room, all trainers are to be completely silent. The dolphin begins experimenting by walking around the room, picking up objects, sitting, standing, etc.

As soon as the dolphin makes any movement whatsoever that brings him or her closer to the desired task, the group collectively says "DING!"

Progress towards the goal is completely achieved through positive direction. There's no groaning or chastising as the dolphin experiments, and at times moves *away* from the goal. There is only silence and dinging.

Now, I must caution you in advance, should you attempt this game with your group (please do! It's such an excellent learning tool!). You'll need to be firm up front about *rogue dingers*. You know: the folks who say *ding* any old time they want. It's confusing for the dolphin when they're confronted with rogue dingers. The dingers must ding in unison.

What I love about this game is its reinforcement of the power of positive feedback. Every time I introduce it, *most* of the people in the room mare skeptical about the outcomes. Every single time, the dolphins are able to figure out the desired task.

A great way to see more of the behavior you want in the people around you is to notice the times when they're doing the desired behavior and acknowledge it.

This game also gives every participant the opportunity to practice critical skills for staying in alignment and participating in effective teamwork. The dolphin gets the chance to practice trusting the process of playful experimentation, and trusting their "trainers" to guide them well. The trainers get to practice trusting the process of offering simple, positive feedback; in return they get an excellent reminder of just how smart the dolphins are. The game requires vulnerability. It's *hard* to be the dolphin and have a group of people with very definite expectations staring at you silently while you do "silly" things in a professional situation.

It's also hard to be the trainer! It's not easy to silently watch someone struggle, feel frustrated, and forget a lesson you thought they learned. People *regularly* beg me to give the dolphins clues.

I never do. Sometimes the dolphin needs a pep talk, or needs to be reminded of the rules of the game... but the dolphin *does not need help figuring out what to do.*

The Dolphin Trainer Game is often a roller coaster of emotions for the participants. It's not uncommon for people to cry—tears of frustration or laughter! That tension makes the pay off so much sweeter; the immense relief and thrill when the dolphin figures out the task is unparalleled. When coached effectively, this game yields big-time breakthroughs for everyone.

CHAPTER SUMMARY

There are three key ways your forgiveness work will manifest itself outwardly at work:

You will shift your dominant intention to be fully supportive of your scene partners, and you'll rest in full trust that the needs of the "audience," AKA the needs of your clients, investors, etc., will be met *even better* through that shift in focus.

You will engage confrontation directly and effectively by entering with forgiveness first, armed only with a party hat and your inner alignment. Confrontation isn't just about disagreement; it's about vulnerability, and the courage someone is tapping into in order to speak up. Confrontation is the *birthplace* of meaningful culture and should be honored and engaged as such.

You will be purposeful and direct about culture expectations, and you will readily hold everyone accountable to that vision and those values. Sometimes this means parting ways with a scene partner. Other times, you can provide necessary support and coaching using the *MIAMI* method of mindful improv and motivational interviewing.

CHAPTER 6: BIGGER THAN ALL OF US

"I alone cannot change the world,
but I can cast a stone across the waters to create many ripples."

~ Mother Teresa

In September of 2016, Kyle and I were in LA visiting my sweet cousin, Carrie, and celebrating our last childless vacation. We knew a foster care placement was on the horizon and a *baby moon* was in order.

It was a beautiful late summer evening, and we had stopped for dessert crepes before catching a show at The Groundlings. As we sat on the patio enjoying our crepes and the beautiful Southern California weather, we noticed a man and woman exiting an SUV not far from our table. The woman was pushing a stroller with a fluffy white dog inside, and the man was carrying a folder full of one-page handouts.

The man got to work quickly, approaching people on the sidewalk and at nearby tables. From a distance, I could vaguely make out that he was unhappy with the government and determined to *stop the lies.*

I watched, intrigued.

Before long he approached a table full of very young adults, maybe even high schoolers. They were polite, but their body language was tense and uncomfortable. As an improviser, social worker, and person who was extremely curious, I decided to hop over and put the kids out of their misery.

The man was a self-described "Flat Earth Theorist." Evidently, he had amassed quite the YouTube following, and he urged me to subscribe to his channel and have all of my questions answered.

I had so many questions. In addition to meeting an alleged YouTube celebrity, never in my life had I encountered someone who believed the Earth was flat!

"This is my first time to meet a Flat Earth Theorist," I said flatly. (When I typed that sentence, there was no pun intended...but now that I see it, the pun IS intended.) "Can you walk me through the basic principles?"

His eyes sparkled with delight. "How did you get here?" he asked. "Did you drive here or did you fly?"

"I flew," I answered.

"Perfect! And let me ask you *this.*" he replied with growing conviction. "Did you fly in a *curve,* or did you fly *in a straight line?*"

"Wow! ...umm. I guess I'm not sure."

"Well, you looked out the windows, didn't you? Did the Earth *look* curved to you? Or did it look flat?"

"*It looked FLAT!!*" I said, delighted to be along for the ride. ...and also, it *did* look flat. I wasn't lying!

"EXACTLY! And let me ask you another thing. Right now, in this moment, do you feel like you're spinning?"

My heart fluttered. I knew we were onto something in this conversation. I wasn't sure what yet, and I knew the conversation wouldn't turn out as he hoped … but I could feel a massive revelation coming. I could feel it in my deepest soul.

"I do not! I definitely *do not feel* like I am spinning."

"Here's the thing," he pontificated, "how can we let the government or textbooks, or anyone else tell us something we can SENSE isn't true?!"

"I mean, I believe the Earth is round because of astronauts."

"They work for the government," came the quick reply.

He then gave me one of his handouts. It included a diagram he had sketched of a flat Earth. I still have it, and I've included it in the book resources at andbeyondimprov.com/bookresources. I kept it because this conversation changed my life and helped me tap deeper into who I really am. This conversation completely shifted the path of my life!

Can you guess why?

I didn't convert to believing the Earth is flat. But I had one of the most important revelations of my life on the flight home. *I can't see the curvature of the Earth…but I KNOW the Earth is round.*

A round Earth makes sense to me because of my understanding of gravity. It makes sense to me because of the rhythm of the sunrise and the sunset. It makes sense to me because of the moon and the tides. It makes sense to me, because of things that are more complicated than what I feel like getting into with a stranger on the sidewalk… but are nevertheless *factual realities.*

I can't feel myself spinning, but I'm thankful for that! How nauseating would that be?!

The truth I stumbled upon is that we cannot see, feel, or detect EVERYTHING that is true in any given moment. All of that sensory input would drive us mad! But our ability to detect the whole truth, and our decision of whether or not to believe in it, has no bearing whatsoever on the truth's existence. Like... *none at all*.

The Earth isn't struggling to be round because a guy with several thousand YouTube followers is convinced otherwise. The tides aren't missing a shift because people doubt the gravitational pull of the moon as it orbits the Earth.

That's just not how *truth* works. It's still true whether or not you're tapped in. Sometimes our sensory input indicates something contradictory to the truth: *I don't feel like I'm on a spinning rock that's hurling in its orbit through outer space. I feel like I'm in a Starbucks listening to a Brené Brown TED talk, and that's the end of my sensory input in this moment.*

If the evidence we have contradicts our bigger truth, we have to hold on to our deeper understanding. This revelation has helped me build meaningful, non-superficial relationships with people whom I had previously assigned labels: bigot, racist, self-righteous a-hole, etc.

The Task is NOT to Agree

I am a woman of faith. My faith is hard for some people to understand. *How can you be a woman of faith who says the F word and has tattoos and enjoys the more-than-occasional libation[23]? How can you be a Mennonite if you don't believe Jesus is the only way to avoid Hell? YOU DON'T BELIEVE IN HELL?!!!*

I used to think I owed people an explanation. I used to think the only way for me to have a relationship with God was for the people in my family and home culture to know exactly what I did and did not believe, and give me their official stamp of approval.

But I know better now. I know who I am.

I *am* a woman of faith: faith in a God beyond the God anyone can name. I have two small Mennonite home churches – one in Canton and one in Pittsburgh. I love them -- those people are my family. I read the Bible. I meditate. I perform in dive bars and comedy theaters. I talk about things that matter to me with people who see the world differently than I do. I get into nature as often as possible. I snuggle my kids at night. I go on 4-day solo vacations.

Let me tell you something: God shows up in all of those places. Regularly. Every time I'm looking in fact. It's okay with me if some people in mainstream Christianity don't get that. It's okay if my atheist friends don't get it. *I finally understand that it's not my job to make you get it!*

It's also not your job to try and see things from my point of view. Peace does not require agreement; it requires *respect* and *acceptance*. Hear that. Because respect and acceptance are different than *tolerance*. I can feel when I'm in the room with people who are tolerating me, and I'm sure you can, too.

---

[23] You'll notice there were no F words in this entire book. That was for your benefit, Aunt B. Yeah, you know who you are. You're welcome. Also, I love you. I know we do life differently, but you are truly one of my heroes.

If we want to be instruments of peace--and oh how I long to be an instrument of peace--we have to do better than "tolerance." We can do better by remembering with 100% confidence that *two things can be true at the same time.*

For example, someone can cut you off in traffic and still be an incredibly loving person with whom you could share a deep and lasting connection. Someone can honk and flip you off for crossing the street while texting, and also be a trusted member of your improv team who didn't recognize you…I'll let you guess if that's a real-life example or not. (It is.)

Someone can vote for a candidate you despise and still have a deeply rooted desire to create more love, peace, acceptance, and safety in the world. Someone can disagree with you about Roe v. Wade and still be a treasured advocate alongside you in creating a world that works for all of us.

I DIDN'T KNOW TERRORISTS COULD PAINT

My very first intentionally productive confrontation happened in an art museum in 2012. I had recently heard an NPR story about asking the question *"What did you mean by that?"* when encountering racism in real life. I've never been more grateful for NPR in my entire life[24].

I was with a dear friend whom I'll call Katie. Katie and I had been friends as long as I can remember. She's a little older than I am, and I've always looked up to her. I still do. Living on opposite

---

[24] *What to Say in the Face of Offensive Remarks.* Talk of the Nation with Jennifer Ludden. July 19, 2012. https://www.npr.org/2012/07/19/157052846/what-to-say-in-the-face-of-offensive-remarks

sides of the country had created some distance in our relationship as adults, but I had been anticipating my trip to visit her and was overjoyed the time had finally come!

Shortly after entering the museum, we found a painting by a Palestinian artist. Katie leaned over to me and said "I didn't know terrorists could paint."

Katie and I grew up in the same conservative, Protestant, evangelical culture that was Zionistic to the point of total disregard of the Palestinian people and the horrific things they've endured. Some even go so far as to say "Palestine doesn't exist."

Her words felt like a punch in the chest; but the truth is that had this been four years earlier, I would have chuckled along with her.

My worldview had expanded because the college I attended requires every student to study abroad. One of the programs they offer is a summer semester in Israel-Palestine. I didn't attend that program, but I was fortunate to live with several people who did.

When they shared with me about their plans to enroll in that program, I feared for their safety. At that time, Israel-Palestine seemed to be the most dangerous place in the world. Weekly, we heard about clashes at the border, and the horrific conditions and violence in the West Bank and the Gaza Strip. I couldn't imagine how my friends could visit there and return in one piece.

When we reunited for the fall semester, I could hardly wait to hear every detail. What I learned was completely shocking to me. In addition to the heartbreaking realities of war, my friends also experienced incredible beauty, joy, and courage.

Furthermore, they returned with a perspective on the conflict I had never heard before. My friends had stayed in the homes of both Palestinian and Jewish families. They crossed the "cottage cheese like border" between Israel-Palestine repeatedly, an experience I found especially harrowing. They said the Palestinian people were incredibly kind and hospitable, and that there was more overlap between Christianity, Judaism, and Islam than I realized.

Had it not been for the willingness of my friends to educate me based on their experiences, I wouldn't know the Palestinian perspective. I would never have heard about *cyclical oppression*, and I certainly wouldn't know that, while innocent people were being victimized on *both* sides of the Israeli-Palestinian conflict, the Palestinians have born the lion's share of brutality and hardship.

I wouldn't have known this if my friends had been scared off by my very narrow and politically charged view of the situation. So; while my initial emotional reaction to Katie's words was one of fear, sadness and anger...how could I *not* pay forward the gift my friends (and NPR) had given me?

"Katie, what did you mean by that?" I asked sincerely.

"Oh... you know," she started.

I stayed quiet to let her finish her thought.

"I mean, aren't the Palestinians the ones basically destroying the Middle East?"

I took a deep breath. "Katie, is it okay if I share with you something I learned recently?"

"Of course!" she said with such genuine love, which is *so typical Katie,* by the way.

I shared with her about my friends' experiences in Israel-Palestine. I shared with her about the Abrahamic roots of Islam, and the very literal reality of the song "Father Abraham had many sons.[25]" We sat down on the floor of the museum and talked for twenty minutes about the pain of the Palestinian people, the vast common ground between Christians, Jews, and Muslims, and how sad it is that politics had invaded our church to the point where we felt pressure to step outside of our loving natures so we could "stick to the party line" on this incredibly complicated and delicate issue.

Katie opened up the Bible App on her phone and fact checked some of the Biblical history I shared with her. We had a conversation that surprised us both! We opened up about our families, our home churches, and the ways in which we wanted to be more loving than some of the beliefs we'd been handed allowed for.

We stood up and Katie hugged me -- tight. It was a *real hug,* between two people who had both just been extremely vulnerable.

It's vulnerable to confront someone about something contentious, but it's also vulnerable to *learn in front of someone.* I'm choked up as I recount this story. It was the first of many more conversations that brought us both closer to the loving source within us.

---

[25] The lyrics of this song: "Father Abraham had many sons. Many sons had Father Abraham. I am one of them, and so are you. So let's all praise the Lord." Growing up, that was a popular children's song in our church. The irony of children learning that song while also learning to hate and fear Muslims is not lost on me.

We walked past the Palestinian artist's piece again, and Katie said "That's a beautiful painting." ...and then we kept walking into a room dedicated to photo documentation of the Civil Rights Movement.

I love that woman. And museums.

THE MORAL OF THE STORY

You may look at someone's attitude, beliefs, or behaviors and see concrete evidence about the *kind of person* they are. You may see an enemy. You may see a dangerous person to be feared. You may see the perpetual thorn in your side who is interrupting your efforts to build a culture that consistently represents and honors your values.

But there is a broader perspective available to you. There is a bigger picture and a deeper understanding. There are shared values and experiences. *There is love at your core and theirs, and you can tap into it to find a way forward.*

That's the heart of mindful improv. That's what helps us trust our aligned instincts and make it our dominant intention to honor our scene partners. That's what gives us the courage and ability to confront and provide accountability when it's necessary.

Mindful improv is impactful for effective leadership, employer branding, employee engagement, and many other work-y, corporate-y, leadership-y things.

But Mindful Improv can do much more than that.

Really, everything in this book is about equipping peacemakers. The founding mantra of my company, &Beyond, is:

Love is the source. Improv is the method. <u>Peace</u> is the outcome.

The goal of this work is nothing short of WORLD PEACE.

That lofty statement is based in the reality that peace is achieved one salvaged relationship at a time. One conscious choice to understand another's perspective. One conscious choice to listen beyond your comfort zone. One conscious choice to prioritize connection over establishing dominance (which is also a key understanding of servant leadership).

Mindful Improv equips us to do all of those things.

My deepest intention for all the things I create--every workshop, leadership development program, retreat, keynote address, YouTube video, and the book you're holding in your hands--is that they contribute to this greater vision for establishing peace.

I decided to focus my peace work in corporate environments for three reasons:

Employers have a huge impact on their employees' sense of joy, freedom, and security, but they don't always know how to be good stewards of that opportunity. Often, the understanding of HOW to be good stewards of the opportunity dilutes as the company grows.

I know what it feels like to be miserable at the hands of a leader who was likely unintentional in their misery-inducing behavior. You probably know what that feels like, too. Work misery bleeds into the rest of your life and makes it really hard to be the parent, partner, professional, or peacemaker you intend to be. Therefore, helping leaders and team members join together to prevent work misery is an ideal way to create more peace in the world. Leaders and team members do this by taking ownership of their own behavior, and readily confronting and providing accountability for one another.

We spend MUCH of our adult lives at work... that means our workplaces have an incredible opportunity to be a training ground for peacemaking behavior. If work is a place where folks can learn and practice how to confront one another honorably, advocate for themselves effectively and respectfully, identify their own biases in service of inclusive collaboration, give and receive feedback graciously, and forgive themselves and each other for the times their actions didn't match their intentions—then we're well on our way to enabling a more empathetic, productive and peaceful society.

As a leader, HR team member, or culture stakeholder, you have an incredible opportunity. That opportunity is bigger than the product you're building at work. It's bigger than the bottom line, though culture and the bottom line are tied together.

You have the opportunity to be a peacemaker—to truly make the world a better place—by the way you lead.

You have the opportunity to positively impact the lives of your employees for the duration of their employment with you, and beyond.

You have the opportunity to help your employees embrace their differences and work together to build something they're proud of.

You have the opportunity to speak truth into your employees' lives at times when they're vulnerable and navigating uncertainty in their personal lives. You have the opportunity to provide the resources that could ultimately improve, or even save, their lives.

You have the opportunity to give people the feedback and coaching that can help them get out of their own way and succeed at a higher caliber than they ever imagined.

This is what Mindful Improv is about: true human connection. Mindful Improv doesn't just inspire us towards a vague, nice-sounding professional utopia. It is also *instructive* on how to reach our culture goals.

Mindful Improv teaches us:

- Proactive curiosity
- Attentive listening
- Sacrificial support of your scene partner
- Present focus
- Unconditional optimism
- Inclusive collaboration
- Self-efficacy
- Forgiveness and resilience

While all of this will most certainly equip your team to navigate change together, collaborate more effectively, and stay with your company longer... the extended impact is that Mindful Improv also equips YOU and your team to actively contribute to a more peaceful world.

If reading those words causes your heart to swell with joy and optimism--and then immediately crash and burn when you consider the reality of complicated workplace relationships or dynamics--keep in mind that you don't need everyone on board in order to get started.

The work starts with you. The work starts with *your* mindful presence in your own story.

That's how you start the work of building lasting, effective culture change. That's how you find inner peace. That's how we change the world together!

It's my second-most-sincere hope that this book has given you helpful ideas on how to be a part of the story of restoration in your office, in the world, and in your own life. My first-most-sincere hope is that you close this book *now* and go play your part in creating the world you want to live in.

You don't need a blueprint. You'll have everything you need when you step forward in alignment. Trust the process of mysterious unfolding. Trust your scene partners. Trust yourself.

You are courageous, capable, willing and worthy.

ABOUT THE AUTHOR

Andrea Flack-Wetherald is a Canton, OH native who lived in Pittsburgh for 11 years before returning to Ohio with her husband and two children. She holds a BSW from Bluffton University and spent the early part of her career working on a research project focused on addiction-related behavior change. This is where her love and appreciation for motivational interviewing was born.

She was introduced to improv through watching *Whose Line Is It Anyway* in middle school and high school, and gained training and performance experience as an adult in Pittsburgh and New York City. Eventually, Andrea got curious about the overlap between an improviser's ability to joyfully listen and collaborate in an ever changing environment and the scientific aspects of optimism and behavior change she learned as a research assistant. Investigating that overlap was the genesis of Andrea's company, &Beyond.

Andrea's work now borrows elements from both fields: the evidence-based methods studied by scientists in the helping professions, and the very practical skills improvisers use to build an entire world in front of your eyes with nothing but imagination and each other. The result is *mindful improv thinking.*

Her work has grown to focus intensively on building healthy, people-first cultures by teaching leaders how to be who they mean to be consistently. There are several ways you can bring Mindful Improv Thinking™ to your group:

- Mindful Improv for Teams: five week virtual program that builds a shared language for brave conversations, self-advocacy and conflict engagement.
- Book Andrea as an event or retreat speaker

More information about these offering at: andbeyondimprov.com.

If you'd like to continue learning Mindful Improv Thinking™ individually, inquire about 1:1 coaching availability via the Contact form on my website. You can also join The Mindful Improv Community - a global network of teachers, pastors, corporate executives, community activists and heart-centered humans holding a beautiful vision for making the world a braver, kinder and safer place. You can join our online community for free via the link on my website.

MINDFUL IMPROV GLOSSARY

Here are some words I use in the book that may warrant a definition. Some of these words have multiple definitions; in that case, I've provided the one representing my usage of the word in this book.

Alignment - Having balance across the pillars of The Trust Tripod: yourself, your scene partner, and the process.

Amy Grant - Greatest living musician of all time; singer of hymns and pop culture favorites like "Baby, Baby" and "Heart in Motion." Fortunately, some of these treasures have been remixed for all of your dancing and workout needs. Also fortunately, they are available on Spotify. If and when you immediately look these up, feel free to tag me in any and all dance videos you post on social media.

Black out - When the lights go out in the theater, indicating the end of a scene. Sometimes we use the term "black out" to refer to a very short sketch that is essentially comprised of one joke.

Box Breathing - A method of mindful breathing in which you inhale for four seconds, hold the breath for four seconds, exhale for four seconds, and then hold the breath again for four seconds

Button - This is the final joke of a scene, or the line delivered by a performer that ties everything together.

Call back - A reference to something that happened earlier in the show

Confrontation – Goes beyond simply understanding a conflict as a *disagreement*. I consider confrontation to be the art of addressing differing opinions or perspectives. Something can be a confrontation without being an *argument,* for example.

Conflict Engagement - I use this term instead of *conflict resolution,* because the prospect of *resolving* conflict on some of the most challenging topics we experience as humans is very intimidating. The average person believes they have no control whatsoever over the trajectory of racism, sexism, or even war. Rather than aiming to resolve conflict, I think it's much more approachable to talk about *engaging*; that's bite-sized. I may not be able to solve the problem of LGBTQ phobia in the church, for example… but I can engage the conversation, and foster growth in myself and others.

Creative Impulse - Inspiration to take specific action that is born out of alignment and takes us closer to realizing our ultimate goals and intentions.

Edit - To end a scene. Often a scene is edited via black out, or an improviser running across the front of the stage, although there are many kinds of scene edits. I use this term for real-life improv moments when we must decide that a conversation, or even a relationship, is over. Just like in improv on stage, characters and themes can be revisited later "in the show" when we've had more time to develop key ideas, or when we're freshly inspired by new developments.

EFT tapping - Emotional Freedom Technique. This is a mindful self-healing technique in which you gently tap various acupressure points on your head, face, neck, and chest while acknowledging the negative or limiting beliefs you're holding about yourself. You say them out loud in this format: "Even though <u>\<insert negative self belief\></u>, I fully and completely love and accept myself." I learned this method from a mindset and business coach, and it was such a powerful example of "Yes, And"-style healing that I've taught it to all of my coaching clients.

Empathy - Most commonly, this is understood as the ability to understand the feelings and/or perspective of another person. When I'm talking with leaders, I encourage them to understand empathy as verb as well a noun. Meaning; what will you *do* about your understanding of another's feelings?

Forgiveness - The ability to look to the future feeling fully empowered, having let go of limiting beliefs about what you can be, do, and have which were formed from past painful and/or traumatic situations.

Green room - The area back stage where performers prepare before a show.

Improv - A form of live comedy in which everything is made up on the spot.

Initiation - The very first thing said by a performer on stage to begin a scene. Initiations should provide the other improvisers with some context for *where* the scene is allegedly taking place and *who they are to each other*. A strong initiation is specific enough to provide the other improvisers with some inspiration to build on, but simple enough to be shaped by the other players.

Long form - A style of improv in which the team gets a suggestion from the audience and performs a series of scenes or a short play inspired by that suggestion. As with all forms of improv, there is no script and everything is made up on the spot.

Mindfulness - The ability to be fully present in the current moment, fully acknowledging your thoughts, feelings, and surroundings, and exploring them with curiosity instead of judgment.

Scene partner - Anyone with whom you are improvising in a given moment, on or off stage. Your mom is your scene partner if that's who you're talking to. Your boss, neighbor, or spouse are also scene partners. I use this term for performance improv and real-life improv!

Scene work - How you are building a scene; the choices you make and the way you initiate or lay back in a scene. I use this term to recall scene work I witnessed or participated in at an actual comedy theater, and scene work I engaged in off stage, too. *All of life is improv, so everything we're doing every day is scene work!*

Self-Efficacy - One's own internal motivation and ability to achieve a goal.

Short form - A style of improv that includes a series of games, similar to what you may have seen on *Who's Line Is It Anyway*. The games often include multiple suggestions, or *gets*, from the audience.

Spirit of Play - The ability to stay in a playful, collaborative headspace despite the happenings of the day. This is the ideal mindset for effective improv; it is light, joyful and collaborative. Hearing one of my former improv coaches use this term inspired me to create The Trust Tripod, which is effectively this mindset in visual format.

Trigger - Specifically, *trauma trigger*; a-response to something that has reminded you of a past traumatic experience.

Zyzzyva - A type of tropical weevil. Found absolutely nowhere in this book; I learned that this is alphabetically the last word in the English language. You're welcome for that knowledge. Consider it a bonus gift for reading this book all the way to the end. You're a real hero. Now go write a review on Amazon, because I self-published this baby and reviews are exceedingly helpful!

Made in the USA
Middletown, DE
16 September 2024

60463253R00128